A CONNECTICUT YANKEE IN KING ARTHUR'S COURT

NOTES

including
- *Life of the Author*
- *Introduction to the Novel*
- *A Brief Plot Summary*
- *List of Major Characters*
- *Summaries and Critical Commentaries*
- *Twain's Method of Characterization*
- *Questions for Review*
- *Selected Bibliography*

by
L. David Allen, Ph.D.
University of Nebraska

and

James L. Roberts, Ph.D.
Department of English
University of Nebraska

Cliffs®Notes
INCORPORATED
LINCOLN, NEBRASKA   68501

Editor

Gary Carey, M.A.
University of Colorado

Consulting Editor

James L. Roberts, Ph.D.
Department of English
University of Nebraska

ISBN 0-8220-0324-4
© Copyright 1982
by
C. K. Hillegass
All Rights Reserved
Printed in U.S.A.

1989 Printing

Cliffs Notes, Inc.   Lincoln, Nebraska

CONTENTS

CONTENTS

A CONNECTICUT YANKEE IN KING ARTHUR'S COURT NOTES

LIFE OF THE AUTHOR

As one of America's first and foremost realists and humorists, Mark Twain, the pen name of Samuel Langhorne Clemens, usually wrote about his own personal experiences and things he knew about from firsthand experience. Two of his best-known novels typify this trait: in his *Adventures of Tom Sawyer*, Twain immortalized the sleepy little town of Hannibal, Missouri (the fictional St. Petersburg), as well as the steamboats which passed through it daily; likewise, in *Adventures of Huckleberry Finn* (both written before *A Connecticut Yankee*), the various characters are based on types which Twain encountered both in his hometown and while working as a riverboat pilot on the Mississippi River; and even though *A Connecticut Yankee* is not based on personal experience (it is set in sixth-century England), Twain uses many of the same techniques that he used in his *Prince and the Pauper*. In that novel, for example, two young boys gradually lose their innocence; in *A Connecticut Yankee*, Hank Morgan wakes up in a land of innocence – Camelot.

Mark Twain's father was a lawyer by profession, but he was never quite successful, and so he dabbled in land speculation, hoping to become wealthy someday. He was, however, a highly intelligent man who was a stern disciplinarian. Twain's mother, a southern belle in her youth, had a natural sense of humor, and was known to be particularly fond of animals and unfortunate human beings. Although his family was not wealthy, Twain apparently had a happy childhood. Twain's father died when Twain was twelve years old and, for the next ten years, Twain was an apprentice printer, both in Hannibal and in New York City. Hoping to find his fortune, he conceived a wild scheme of getting rich in South America. On a riverboat to New Orleans, however, he met a famous riverboat pilot who promised to teach him the trade for five hundred dollars. After completing his training, Twain was a riverboat pilot for four years and, during this time, he became familiar with all of the towns along the Mississippi River.

When the Civil War began, Twain's allegiance tended to be somewhat southern due to his regional heritage, but his brother Orion convinced him to go west on an expedition, a trip which became the subject of a later work *Roughing It*. Even though some of his letters and accounts of traveling had been published earlier, Twain actually launched his literary career with the short story "The Notorious Jumping Frog of Calaveras County," published in 1865.

Because of the acclaim of *Roughing It*, Twain gave up his career as a journalist-reporter and began writing seriously. His fame as a writer was immediate; one of his first efforts, *Innocents Abroad*, became an immediate best seller, and it is still one of his most popular works. The satire that Twain uses to expose the so-called sophistication of the Old World, in contrast to the old-fashioned Yankee common sense, is similar to that found some years later in *A Connecticut Yankee*, when Hank Morgan confronts nobility and knighthood. But it was the Mississippi River and the values of the people who lived along its length that have made Twain one of America's best and favorite storytellers. The humor which he found there, along with its way of life, has continued to fascinate readers and to embody an almost mythic sense of what it meant to be a young American in the latter part of the nineteenth century.

After Twain turned fifty, however, his fortunes reversed themselves; his health began to fail and he faced bankruptcy; in addition, his wife became a semi-invalid, one daughter developed epilepsy, and his oldest daughter died of meningitis. Yet Twain survived. He became a critic and an essayist, and he became more popular as a satirist than as a humorist. The body of work which he left behind is immense and varied—poetry, sketches, journalistic pieces, political essays, novels, and short stories—all a testament to the diverse talent and energy which used the folklore of frontier America to create authentic American masterpieces of enduring value.

INTRODUCTION TO THE NOVEL

There are two approaches to *A Connecticut Yankee*: there are the numerous polemic digressions on such weighty subjects as social criticism on slavery, on the injustices of the Church and the nobility, on the absurdity of hereditary preferments, on the ridiculousness of knighthood, and on the existence of unjust laws. However, conjointly, we also have a very fanciful story (bordering on science fiction) which delights the reader with its inventiveness.

A Connecticut Yankee, interestingly, has frequently been referred to as Twain's most "magnificent failure." Of course, the novel is not a failure, but what has troubled many critics is the fact that the novel contains at least two major concerns and these concerns, at times, seem to contradict each other.

The first basic contradiction occurs when Hank Morgan, a representative of Nineteenth-Century Progress, is thrown back into the sixth century, where he is supposed to use his Yankee ingenuity and inventiveness to remove the barbaric ignorance and superstitions of that inhumane and unjust world. He is supposed to enlighten and improve these "innocent" people through the use of his modern skills and the inventions and political views of his time, but, finally, he not only fails, but he destroys, in large measure, a beautiful civilization (Camelot) that existed so peacefully and idyllically before his arrival.

The second contradiction occurs upon Morgan's return to the nineteenth century. In the final chapter, we hear him ranting and raving; his deathbed wish is to be permitted to return to his Camelot, his "lost land," his home, and his friends; he wants to be allowed to return to "all that is dear . . . all that makes life worth the living." His last wish is to rejoin his wife, Sandy, and their child, Hello-Central. When he thinks that he holds her, he thinks that all is well: "All is peace, and I am happy again."

Consequently, every judgment against Camelot, every harsh statement concerning the conditions of Camelot, every condemnation rendered against the entire feudal society of sixth-century England and all other objections are contradicted by Hank Morgan's nostalgic longings to return to that happy and innocent land.

We have, therefore, two different views throughout the novel; we have Twain's own condemnations of certain aspects of feudal England, and we have Hank Morgan's nostalgic longing for the beauty of a pure, simple, and innocent society. This is illustrated throughout the novel in many ways. There are long polemic digressions against knight-errantry, and alongside these digressions, Twain details the positive, chivalric nobility of Sir Launcelot. We hear other condemnations against the concept of monarchy, including the idea that when two people are dressed alike, no one can tell the difference between a commoner and a royal personage. In contradiction, Hank Morgan constantly reiterates the fact that no matter what one may do, one cannot disguise the fact that King Arthur has royal blood and a spirit that cannot be humbled or brought to yoke. Many more examples such as these inform the entire novel. Thus, it is for these reasons that the novel is often referred to as a "magnificent failure" — that is, Twain's social criticism is brilliant and pointed; Hank Morgan's view of Camelot, however, does not agree with the criticisms which Twain levels against Camelot and its institutions.

The subject matter of *A Connecticut Yankee* appealed to Twain because it was an age controlled by nobility and royalty, a subject which Twain enjoyed deriding. But in most of his novel, Twain was always fascinated by the concept of an innocent people dwelling in an innocent society. Furthermore, the subject matter of *A Connecticut Yankee* allowed Twain to specifically utilize his vast knowledge of history and biography, two subjects which occupied much of Twain's reading time; in addition, writing this novel allowed Twain the opportunity to meditate on the injustices inherent in human nature (or "the damned human race" as it was so termed in his later work, *The Mysterious Stranger*). The subject matter of this novel also allowed Twain to indulge in one of his favorite pastimes — using a language different from that used by either the common people or the educated people; the idioms and dialects of *Tom Sawyer* and *Huck Finn* and the archaic language of *The Prince and the Pauper* and *A Connecticut Yankee* are all illustrations of Twain's penchant for utilizing different sorts of language.

A BRIEF PLOT SUMMARY

A Connecticut Yankee in King Arthur's Court is a "framed story." That is, the first chapter tells how a tourist in England, presumably Mark Twain, meets a stranger who tells him part of his story and then gives him a manuscript that tells the rest of his strange tale. In the last chapter, the tourist has finished reading the manuscript and searches out the stranger, only to find him dying and calling out for the wife and daughter whom he had lived with in sixth-century England.

In the first chapter, this stranger (we later learn that his name is Hank Morgan, but he is usually referred to in the novel as The Boss) tells the tourist that he was something of a jack-of-all-trades who had a particular aptitude for making and inventing things mechanical. He is from Hartford, Connecticut, where he had been head superintendent in a munitions factory until, in a fight with one of the workers, he was hit in the head with a crowbar. When he awakened, he was sitting in the grass under a tree. A man in old-fashioned armor took him prisoner, and they rode off to what Hank Morgan believed would probably be an insane asylum. At this point in the story, this stranger begins to feel very sleepy, so he gives the tourist the manuscript detailing his adventures, which he has written from the journals that he kept.

The first chapter of the manuscript (the introductory chapter is technically a prologue) begins with the knight and Hank Morgan riding through a quiet countryside that Morgan does not recognize. After a time, they arrive in a small, wretched town and pass through the gates of a huge castle; they then enter into a great paved court.

Trying to find out what asylum this is, Hank Morgan talks with a young man who tells him that the year is 528 and that the day is June 19; Morgan has been captured by Sir Kay the Seneschal, and he will be exhibited before the court. Then he will be sent to the dungeons to either rot or be ransomed.

At the feast around the Round Table, Sir Kay's turn to tell of his adventures finally arrives, but he is interrupted by Merlin, who tells the story of how King Arthur got his sword from the Lady of the Lake; he puts the entire crowd to sleep. When Sir Kay does tell his story, he exaggerates immensely. Then Arthur sentences Morgan to die at noon on the 21st. Morgan is stripped of his "enchanted" clothes and is hauled off to the dungeons.

When Clarence (the boy to whom he had talked) comes to visit him, Morgan tells the boy to take a message to the court; he says that he is a magician more powerful than Merlin. The message has some effect, but Merlin ultimately scoffs at the claims of this "magician" because the so-called spell that Morgan says that he will cast is not specified. By this time, Morgan has remembered that there will be an eclipse of the sun at noon on the 21st, so Morgan sends Clarence back to tell the court that he will blot out the sun – if he must.

Shortly thereafter, Morgan is hauled out to the courtyard and chained to a stake. A monk is praying for him when, suddenly, he stops, and Morgan notices that the solar eclipse is just beginning. He realizes that when he asked Clarence what day it was, Clarence gave him the incorrect day. Thus Morgan puts his knowledge of the eclipse to good use, thereby gaining his freedom and a position as "perpetual minister and executive" to the king, as well as liberal funding, if he will "let" the sun shine again. He keeps the king and the knights in suspense for a time, ostensibly to make sure that the king meant what he said; then, when he notices that the eclipse is total, he announces that his spell will now begin to pass away.

This "miracle" makes Morgan a man of great interest to the people of the kingdom, and when Merlin begins spreading rumors about him, Morgan blows up Merlin's tower, using explosives which he and Clarence have made. This "miracle" solidifies Morgan's position in the country.

At one of the frequent tournaments held in Camelot, Sir Dinadan (who tells many bad jokes) is being drubbed by Sir Gareth, and The Boss (as Morgan is now called) says that he hopes that he (Sir Dinadan) dies. By the time these ambiguous words are uttered, however, Sir Gareth has crashed into Sir Sagramor le Desirous, and Sir Sagramor thinks that Morgan's derogatory wish was meant for him. Sagramor therefore challenges Morgan, The Boss, to a bout after he, Sagramor, returns from questing after the Holy Grail. The king and others urge The Boss to also undertake a quest so that he will be more worthy of taking on Sir Sagramor. Morgan puts off this journey for some time, though, so that he can make some changes in the kingdom—such changes as providing some schools, factories, military academies, telephones, and telegraph lines; all these changes are done quietly, of course, so that they will not be too noticeable immediately.

Finally, Morgan can put off his quest no longer. The king decides that Morgan will accompany the Demoiselle Alisande la Carteloise to free her mistress and forty-four princesses held captive by three giants with one eye each.

Along the way, Morgan, The Boss, discovers many things; first, he learns that armor is very uncomfortable to ride in and also to sleep in. Then he and the Demoiselle have a meal with several freemen, one of whom is willing to think about change; as a result, he is sent back to Camelot for Clarence to put into training. A little later, The Boss terrifies six armed knights by stoking up a head of smoke with his pipe as they charge at him; the knights halt, amazed, and are willing to surrender. That evening, the evening of the second day out from Camelot, they come upon the castle ruled by Morgan le Fay. Although the wicked le Fay has a quick temper and is willing to kill anyone who crosses her even slightly, she becomes very deferential when she learns that her visitor is The Boss. She allows him his way even after he frees a man accused of killing a deer on the royal preserve and even though he frees nearly all of the prisoners in her dungeons. She casually stabs for a young boy, but she refrains from throwing his grandmother, who curses her for that deed, into the dungeons.

Several days later, Sandy (the name which Morgan has given his traveling companion) informs The Boss that they are coming upon an ogre's castle. The Boss, however, can see only a pigsty filled with pigs, but Sandy assures him that it *is* a castle and that those *are* princesses (and not pigs) who must be freed. Rather than argue with her, The Boss agrees that this castle must surely be enchanted—but enchanted for his eyes only. Thus, he rides down and buys the pigs from the swineherds. He and Sandy then drive the pigs to a nearby castle, where the "princesses" will wait to be reclaimed by their kin or friends.

When The Boss and Sandy meet a band of pilgrims heading toward the Valley of Holiness, they also decide to travel in that direction. On the way, they meet one of The Boss's "sign board knights," knights who are advertising various products which The Boss wants to introduce into England. But it is not long before they learn that there is a problem in the Valley of Holiness that requires one of the Boss's spells to set right, so he sends a knight back to Camelot with a note to Clarence for supplies and helpers.

The problem in the Valley of Holiness is that the holy well, believed to be the product of a miracle in an earlier day, has gone dry. The Boss examines it and finds that a section of the wall has been broken. While he waits for his supplies and aides to arrive from Camelot, he insists that professional courtesy requires him to wait until Merlin gives up before he takes over. Merlin does finally admit that he has failed to fill the well, but he gives up just as two of The Boss's helpers arrive; when they do, they quickly repair the hole in the well's wall, and then they prepare to make a spectacle of the restoration of water to the well. The "miracle," of course, is a success, and The Boss's reputation is reaffirmed.

A short time later, however, another magician arrives, and for the moment, he eclipses The Boss's reputation. All is not lost, however. Using a telephone that has just been installed in one of the abandoned caves in the Valley, The Boss predicts that the king and his retinue will be in the Valley of Holiness in two days; the other magician insists that the king will be traveling in the other direction. When the king does arrive on time, the other magician is discredited.

While the king is there, he dispenses justice, he oversees the choosing of officers for the standing army (a process that The Boss is unhappy with), and he allows those who are ill to attempt to heal themselves by touching him. After this business is taken care of, The Boss and the king set out to travel into the countryside in disguise. The Boss wants to find out, firsthand, what the conditions of the country are, and the king thinks that it might be a lark to go along. Thus, the two set out.

The Boss and the king have a number of problems on their journey because the king simply will not, or cannot, act like a peasant; indeed, The Boss manages to save them from being killed several times, once by using a dynamite bomb to blow up a group of charging knights.

During one incident, they help a woman who is dying of smallpox, leaving just before her sons, who had been imprisoned by the local lord, escape and arrive home. As The Boss and the king move through the night, they see the glow of a fire in the distance, and they discover the corpses of a number of men who have been hanged. Near morning, they come to a hut, and they finally convince the woman who greets them to give them some hospitality. After they have slept, she feeds them, and they learn that the lord of that area has been killed and that all the freemen in the neighborhood have been out all night looking for whoever is responsible for the murder. The Boss notices that his host and hostess are terribly nervous, and he guesses that they are probably related to the boys who are responsible for the lord's death. Therefore, he goes out with his host, Marco, and they agree that they will say nothing about key suspects who escaped. Instead, they walk through the village talking to people. The Boss invites a number of them to dinner that Sunday, and he insists on paying for everything; thus a sumptuous spread is prepared at the store.

The Boss's purpose in gathering these people for a meal is to find out what they think about wages and about the relationship between wages and purchasing power; he wants to convince them that his way of thinking is better than theirs, but all he manages to do is make them suspicious of him. Then, before he can cover up his error and ease their suspicions, the king begins talking about agricultural matters in such a way that makes these people think that he is mad. As a result, the men set upon the king and The Boss. Although the king and The Boss are winning the fight, they notice that their hosts have left. Suspecting that they have gone for help to aid their neighbors, the king and The Boss flee.

They are finally captured, however, but before these villagers can beat them, as they intend to do, the king and The Boss are rescued by an earl named Grip. Although Grip feeds them, gives them a room for the night, and lends them horses to ride to the next town, once they are there, he has them bound and sold as slaves.

They are then driven to London, along with a number of other slaves. Along the way, they see several instances of the cruelty of the laws and the difficulties of the life of the common people. After a time, The Boss manages to steal a metal clasp with a long pin from a prospective slave buyer; he uses this as a lock pick, and he is able to free himself. Before he can escape, however, the slave master comes in. The Boss tries to catch him, but he scuffles with the wrong man, and both of them are arrested. In the morning, in court, The Boss tells the judge a story that effects his immediate release, and he uses a telephone to call Clarence in Camelot so that knights can be sent to the rescue.

In the meantime, he learns that the slaves had killed the slave-master in the night and that all of them are to be hanged. He tries to make some contacts with people he knows, but in doing so, he is captured and put in with the other slaves; the jailer tells him that they are all to be hanged in the middle of the afternoon.

At a climactic moment when three of the slaves have been hanged, and the blindfold has been put on the king, suddenly five hundred of Camelot's finest knights ride up on bicycles. They take charge of the situation and rescue the king and The Boss.

Just after they return to Camelot, The Boss learns that he must enter the tournament lists and must joust against Sir Sagramor.

Instead of conventional weapons, however, The Boss uses a lasso and ropes Sir Sagramor and yanks several other knights off their horses. After Merlin steals the rope, Sir Sagramor challenges The Boss again; this time, The Boss uses a revolver which he has made and shoots him. When one of the other knights challenges him, The Boss challenges all of them together, and he shoots nine of them before the rest turn and flee.

After this, The Boss has his own way for a time, and he makes many changes in England, revealing some of the earlier changes which he quietly accomplished. He also marries Sandy, and they have a child whom Sandy names Hello-Central. When Hello-Central falls ill, The Boss spends a great deal of time with her and, on the advice of doctors, he takes her to the seaside. She falls ill again while they are visiting a kingdom on the French coast. About a month later, after she is fully recovered, The Boss goes to England to see what has happened to the boat which they had sent to bring them supplies; they are worried, for it should have returned at least three weeks earlier. Once in England, The Boss learns that all of the changes which he had made have now fallen under an Interdict of the Catholic Church.

The Boss then makes his way to Camelot. He and Clarence make plans for a final battle against most of England, with only fifty-two of the people whom they trained as helpers. Working from Merlin's cave, they kill twenty-five thousand knights, using electric fencing, Gatling guns, and an ingeniously diverted stream. When The Boss goes out to see if they can give aid to any of those who still survive, one of the wounded enemies stabs him. Luckily, however, the wound is only slight. Yet all is far from being peaceful yet, for Merlin enters the cave in the guise of an old woman and casts a spell on The Boss that makes him sleep for thirteen hundred years. Thus the novel ends with the tourist's reaching The Boss's room just as The Boss dies, calling for Sandy and Hello-Central.

LIST OF MAJOR CHARACTERS

Mark Twain

Samuel Langhorne Clemens, the author of *A Connecticut Yankee in King Arthur's Court*; he is the tourist to whom Hank Morgan tells part of his story and to whom Morgan gives the manuscript that chronicles his adventures in sixth-century England.

Hank Morgan

The Connecticut Yankee in King Arthur's court. Using his nineteenth-century knowhow, he becomes known as a "magician" in sixth-century England; he tries to bring about many changes in the way of life in that century. Throughout most of the book, he is referred to as The Boss.

Sir Kay the Seneschal

The knight who captures Morgan when he first appears in the sixth century.

Clarence

A page whom Morgan meets when he first arrives in Camelot; he becomes Morgan's first recruit and his second-in-command in Morgan's attempts to change Arthurian England.

Arthur

King of Britain, the ruler in Camelot, and The Boss's companion during an incognito visit among the lower classes of England.

Merlin

Supposedly the mightiest magician of the times, he is bested several times by The Boss; it is he who puts The Boss under a spell that causes him to sleep from the sixth century to the nineteenth century.

Guenever

Queen of England; she is Arthur's wife, although she is much more romantically interested in Sir Launcelot.

Sir Launcelot

He is the most prominent knight of the Round Table, and he is the main cause, along with Guenever, of the Interdict that overtakes England late in the novel.

Sir Sagramor le Desirous

Another knight of the Round Table; he challenges The Boss because of a supposed slight; he is finally shot by The Boss.

Sandy

She is more formally known as the Demoiselle Alisande la Carteloise; she comes to Camelot with a tale about her mistress being held captive by three ogres. King Arthur decides that The Boss will accompany her to set this matter right. Morgan later comes to admire her a great deal and, eventually, he marries her.

Morgan le Fay

Arthur's sister and King Urien's wife; she is the real ruler of their small kingdom, but she is deferential to The Boss, since his reputation as a magician preceded him to her castle.

Marco

He is a charcoal burner; the king and The Boss stay with him and his wife on their incognito tour of the realm; after a while, Marco and his wife become alarmed by the behavior of the king and The Boss, and they go after help against these two strangers.

Dowley

The blacksmith in the village near where the Marcos live; he is a primary target of The Boss's attempts to bring the villagers' thinking about economic matters into line with his.

Grip, an Earl

An important man in the neighborhood where the Marcos live; he and his men rescue the king and the Boss from the villagers, but they sell them into slavery the next day.

Hello-Central

The daughter of The Boss and Sandy; she is given her unusual name when Sandy hears The Boss repeat it frequently in his sleep; she believes that it is the name of one of Morgan's old girlfriends.

Sir Mordred

A nephew of King Arthur. He is the primary cause of the Interdict that wipes out the progress which The Boss has brought to England because he uses the fighting between the king's party and Launcelot's party in the battle over the queen to try and take power himself.

Sir Meliagraunce

A knight wounded in Morgan's last battle; he stabs Morgan, and this allows Merlin to put a spell on Morgan that causes him to sleep thirteen hundred years.

SUMMARIES AND COMMENTARIES

A WORD OF EXPLANATION

Summary

"A Word of Explanation," together with a "Final P. S. by M. T." at the end of the novel, establishes a "frame" for the story of Hank Morgan's adventures in Arthurian England. The narrator in this introductory chapter tells us how he came to hear parts of this story and that he read the rest of the story in a manuscript.

It happened that he was taking a tour through Warwick Castle when he met another man, who began walking with him and began telling him tales about such people as Sir Launcelot of the Lake, Sir Galahad, and other knights of the Round Table. In the course of the tour and the conversation, this man introduces to the narrator the idea of the transpositions of epochs and of bodies. He also mentions that it was he who put a bullet hole in the armor of Sir Sagramor le Desirous. This strange man disappears, however, before the narrator can ask him further questions about any of these subjects.

That evening, the narrator reads a tale from Sir Thomas Malory's famous book, *Le Morte Darthur*; the tale he reads concerns how Sir Launcelot rescues Sir Kay and conquers three other knights in the process. As he finishes the tale, a knock is heard at the door: it is the stranger. After drinking four Scotch whiskeys, this man, whom the narrator met earlier in the day, tells his story.

He is, he says, an American from Hartford, Connecticut, and he is "a Yankee of Yankees." He learned blacksmithing from his father, horse doctoring from his uncle, and all manner of mechanical arts from a job which he had in a factory. Because of his skill in making and inventing things mechanical, he soon became head superintendent of the factory and supervised several thousand men. One day, however, an unfortunate accident occurred; while he was in a fight with one of his fellow employees, he was knocked unconscious with a crowbar.

When he came to, he was sitting in the grass under an oak tree, and then a man in "old-time iron armor from head to heel, with a helmet on his head the shape of a nail keg with slits in it" rode up and challenged him. Not understanding what was going on, the man from Connecticut, the stranger, told the man in armor to get "back to your circus." The knight backed off and lowered his lance, and the stranger climbed the tree. After some argument, the stranger agreed to go with the knight, even though he believed that the man was probably an escapee from a lunatic asylum.

At this point, the stranger seems to be drifting off to sleep, but before he does so, he gives the narrator a manuscript of his adventures, tales which he has written down from journals which he kept. As he leaves the stranger, who is falling asleep, the narrator begins to examine the manuscript; it is written on old, yellowed parchment over "traces of a penmanship which was older and dimmer still — Latin words and sentences: fragments from old monkish legends, evidently." Filled with curiosity, he begins to read.

Commentary

Twain uses the age-old literary device of a "frame" to enclose his story; the use of this device adds a certain degree of credibility to a story which will ultimately be seen as a type of utopia in reverse. Here, there will be a constant double vision of Camelot throughout the narrative. Hank Morgan will try to change everything which he sees, and he will try to bring this medieval civilization up to the "standards" of the nineteenth century, and yet, at the same time, the medieval civilization is presented in idyllic images of innocent people playing charming games, surrounded by an elegant landscape which is colored by pageantry of all types.

In the opening frame, the narrator is touring the ancient Warwick Castle, and when the guide mentions a mysterious hole in one piece of ancient armor and suggests that it must have been done maliciously at a much later date in history, a mysterious stranger announces that he was there when the hole was made. In the opening scene of this novel, then, we have information about the final disposition of Sir Sagramor le Desirous, information which will not fully appear until Chapter 39. But our imagination is caught and our interest in this mystery is sparked. We will not know anything further until many more chapters later, but obviously Twain had his basic plot worked out at the beginning of the frame. Later, the mysterious stranger comes to the narrator's room in the Warwick Arms Hotel with the manuscript; it is aged, written on yellow paper and supposedly it was written thirteen hundred years ago; in addition to the manuscript's seeming to be very old, note that the handwriting looks strained. These facts all add to the suspense, and they also give further "credence" to the story inside the frame.

Whereas many of Twain's other great novels deal with the Mississippi River or the Mississippi River Valley or some other subject matter which he knew well, in this particular novel, *A Connecticut Yankee in King Arthur's Court*, Twain sets his narrative far back in time so as to compare and contrast certain aspects of a long-dead civilization with a modern, industrial one. Hank Morgan, the central character whom Twain chooses for his hero, is perfectly suited for this "transposition of epochs" for several reasons. First, like so many of Twain's narrators, Morgan is one of Twain's innocent people – that is, like Huck Finn, Morgan reports pretty much what he sees. But more important, before his transposition, Morgan has been trained in all sorts of practical matters. The combination of his being associated with both a blacksmith and a horse doctor will serve him well in sixth-century England. More important, his knowledge of "guns, revolvers, cannons, boilers, engines [and] all sorts of labor-saving machinery" will be of the utmost use to him. Furthermore, he can seemingly invent anything; therefore, he is both an inventor and inventive.

The blow on the head that Hank Morgan received in the fight then leaves everything in doubt as to whether or not he was actually back in the sixth century, or whether or not he has dreamed all of these fanciful thoughts. Certainly in the Post Script section, Hank (or The Boss, as he will be called) longs to return not to the nineteenth century but to the sixth century. Thus, in the final analysis, whatever criticism that The Boss makes of Camelot and its civilization, we must remember that at the end of the novel, when Morgan is sick and his mind is rambling, he would prefer Camelot and that century to the one in which he is now living.

Twain's own comments about his Connecticut Yankee help us better understand his intention in writing this novel; he wrote to the illustrator: "This Yankee of mine . . . is a perfect ignoramus; he is boss of a machine shop, he can build a locomotive or a Colt's revolver, he can put up and run a telegraph line, but he's an ignoramus nevertheless." By this, Twain meant that the Yankee was not a person of intellect, but that he was a person of Yankee ingenuity. An intellectual in sixth-century England would not have survived; indeed, it would take an inventive and ingenious person to survive such an incredible, unbelievable time transposition.

CHAPTERS 1 and 2

Summary

As they ride along, the narrator of "A Word of Explanation" notices the quiet of the countryside and the lack of people and wagons. When they meet a young girl, he is surprised that she is calm; seemingly, the man in armor causes no alarm within her; nor does she seem unusually interested in him. But when she sees the narrator, her hands fly up. She is startled and astonished by his appearance. He cannot imagine why *he* would cause such fright and curiosity.

The two men ride on, then, and the town they come to, finally, is a wretched place. The streets are narrow and crooked, the dogs and hogs roam at will, and there is a pervasive stench about the place.

The townsmen have unkempt hair, most of the people wear knee-length robes of coarse tow-linen, and many of them wear iron collars; the children are mostly naked. And again, it is the narrator who draws the astonished stares, not the man in armor.

Suddenly, they hear military music, and soon a noble company in rich clothing rides through the town, paying no attention to the people or the animals. The narrator and his captor follow this procession to a huge castle and into the great paved court.

The narrator — we later learn that his name is Hank Morgan — tries to find out what kind of "asylum" he has come to, and he concludes that the first person whom he talks to is one of the "patients." The second person whom he meets refuses to talk, but he points to "an airy slim boy in shrimp-colored tights." This lad comes up to him and tells him that he is wanted. As they walk, the boy tells Hank that the year is 528, that all the people whom they see are not "patients"; they are in their right minds, and this is King Arthur's court into which he has been brought. The boy also tells him that the day is June 19. From his memory, Hank dredges up the fact that at noon of June 21, 528, there is supposed to be a complete eclipse of the sun. He determines to use this as a test of whether or not he is somehow in the year 528 or in his own year of 1879.

That settled, he decides to make the best of his situation and to find out what he can about it; he also decides that if this really is the sixth century, he is going to take charge and make some changes. Accordingly, he names the boy Clarence. Hank then asks the name of his captor. He is told that the knight is "Sir Kay the Seneschal, foster brother to our liege the king." Clarence also tells Hank that he will be thrown into a dungeon until his friends ransom him, or until he rots, whichever comes first. Before that, however, Hank hears that Sir Kay will show him off to the court and tell the tale of his capture, exaggerating the details.

As they wait for Sir Kay's turn to speak, Hank looks about the place. It is immense and built of ancient stones. There is little ornamentation, except for a few tapestries showing scenes of battle and of men in armor. In the middle of the hall is the Round Table, as large as a circus ring. Around this huge oaken table are "men dressed in such various and splendid colors." They are eating and drinking prodigiously, and one of their diversions is to throw a bone to the dogs surrounding the table and then watch them fight for it. Hank judges that the "speech and behavior of these people [is] gracious and courtly" most of the time, but that "they [are] a childlike and innocent lot," for they believe every lie that someone tells.

He also discovers that he is not the only prisoner waiting to be exhibited and that the others are in much worse shape than he is; most have been severely hacked up and are in great pain, although not a sound of distress is heard from them. He reasons that they must have treated others in like manner; thus, their punishment is something they could expect and prepare for; it is, in other words, a matter of training rather than of philosophy.

Commentary

Chapter 1 begins the narrative proper of the novel. For centuries, Camelot has been the idyllic dream of romantic perfection (even in the twentieth century, one of the most popular Broadway musicals is entitled *Camelot*), thus the fact that Hank Morgan has never heard of Camelot shows him to be grounded in reality and practicality; nothing of the sentimental or romantic will affect him.

Yet part of the dual vision of the novel occurs immediately. Hank's opening description of the landscape suggests that he is affected by the quiet and lovely beauty of the area; thus, the hard-nosed, practical Yankee is placed in an innocent, idyllic land: "It was a soft, reposeful summer landscape, as lovely as a dream, and . . . the air was full of the smell of flowers and the buzzing of insects, and the twittering of birds. . . ." This kind of countryside could belong anywhere in Twain's novels that deal with an innocent person entering into another land; it is very much like Huck Finn's Jackson Island and many other places in Twain's fiction. But Morgan's practicality brings him quickly out of this romantic idyll.

The double view of Camelot and its inhabitants is presented in Chapter 2, and it continues in one form or another throughout the novel. Hank Morgan sees the knights and the royalty as being childish but charming: "As a rule the speech and behavior of these people were gracious and courtly . . . and . . .they were a childlike and innocent lot; telling lies of the stateliest pattern with the most gentle and winning naivete. . . ." Thus, throughout the novel, Hank is charmed by the very people that he is desperately trying to change. Ultimately, Hank Morgan will try to destroy the innocent habits of Camelot, but, ironically, he will, in turn, be destroyed by his own plans. The manner in which these gentle people tell lies in stately patterns is later correlated with the manner in which modern diplomats also tell stately lies in gentle patterns. Thus, the centuries have not changed people in high diplomatic positions very much.

CHAPTERS 3-5

Summary

Around the Round Table, the various knights tell the tales of their prowess at arms. As he watches and listens, Hank decides that there is something lofty, sweet, and manly about these men, but also that they are simplehearted and lacking in brainpower.

Sir Kay is brought to the fore when six prisoners come forward and, to the disbelief of most present, announce that they have been conquered by him. Sir Kay then tells the tale of how they were captured by Sir Launcelot (the tale that the frame narrator read in Malory), as well as other tales of Sir Launcelot's adventures, exaggerating the whole time.

At that point, Merlin — a very old, white-bearded man — stands "upon unsteady legs, and feebly swaying his ancient head [surveys] the company with his watery and wandering eye." Clarence groans and tells Hank that Merlin is about to tell the tale that he always tells when he has gotten drunk. Merlin does, putting most of the court to sleep in the process. His story is about how King Arthur got his sword from the Lady of the Lake.

Sir Dinadan is the first to awaken after Merlin's tale, and he amuses himself by tying metal mugs to a dog's tail. This arouses the other dogs, who chase the first; the noise then awakens all the knights, and they all have a good laugh. After that excitement dies down, Sir Dinadan strings together a number of jokes that Hank has already heard about thirteen centuries later; they were old even in the sixth century.

After this, Sir Kay gets up to tell of his feat at arms. Hank says, "He spoke of me all the time in the blandest way as 'this prodigious giant,' and 'this horrible sky-towering monster,' and 'this tusked and taloned man-devouring ogre,' and everybody took in all this bosh in the naivest way." The other facts of the encounter are likewise stretched. After this tale, Arthur sentences Hank to die at noon on the 21st. There is a discussion of what to do about Hank's enchanted clothes; when Merlin has the sense to suggest that they strip him, they do so immediately. Hank is embarrassed, but everyone else discusses his physique with no hesitation or concern.

Finally, Hank is carried off to the dungeon, but he is so tired that he falls asleep almost as soon as they leave him to himself in the cell. When he awakens, he is sure that everything that has happened to him is a dream. Just then, however, Clarence comes to visit him, which dispels the notion.

After he finally gets it through his head that this is no dream, Hank asks Clarence to help him escape; Clarence, however, thinks that such a feat is impossible because there are so many guards. In addition, Merlin has put a spell on the dungeons, and no one in the kingdom would think of helping anyone escape. Hank, hardheaded Yankee that he is, hoots at the idea of a magic spell, but that gives him an idea: he tells Clarence that he is a magician himself. Furthermore, he claims to be a much more powerful magician than Merlin, and he sends Clarence to let the court know that there will be trouble if anything happens to him.

While Clarence is gone, Hank worries about whether or not it will occur to the boy that a magician wouldn't have to send a boy with this message. (It doesn't.) He also decides to use the eclipse as his piece of magic.

When Clarence returns, he reports that the message had an effect, but that Merlin scoffed because the disaster was not named. Thus Hank sends Clarence back with the message that he will blot out the sun if he must.

Commentary

In Chapter 3, we are introduced to many of the "Knights of the Round Table." We must remember that when Hank Morgan carried his manuscript to the "frame narrator" that the frame narrator was reading from Sir Thomas Malory's *Le Morte Darthur*; Twain himself was exceptionally fond of this old volume and used certain episodes from Malory's book.

The dual perspective of Camelot and its royalty continues in Chapter 3 when Hank Morgan observes: "There was something very engaging about these great simplehearted creatures, something attractive and lovable. There did not seem to be brains enough in the entire nursery, so to speak, to bait a fishhook with." But these are the charming, innocent, and lofty people whom he loves, and yet he will be determined to destroy large numbers (25,000) of them later in order to have his own way—that is, in order to force civilization on them.

Chapter 3 also introduces Merlin, who will function as the antagonist to Hank Morgan. They will be not just rival magicians, but they will also be rivals in all ways.

Chapter 4 emphasizes the childish aspects of the knights—the games that amuse them are games that children still play today—games such as tying a can on the tail of a dog and then laughing to see the dog run, frightened of its own tail. Furthermore, Hank Morgan has to also listen to some dull, flat jokes that he has already heard thirteen hundred years later, only to discover that they were dull and flat in the sixth century also. In both the jokes and in the tales that the knights narrate, there is so much gross exaggeration in them that Hank Morgan finds it incredible that anyone would believe the stories. Yet it is part of the charm of the innocents that they would believe anything that is told to them.

At the end of Chapter 4, Hank Morgan's clothes are removed, at the suggestion of Merlin, and they all comment upon his physique. He is extremely embarrassed both by his nakedness and even more by the language that the ladies use to describe his various naked parts. Later, we discover that essentially Hank Morgan is not just a Yankee, but a Yankee prude. He chides the court for its foul speech, he feels (later) that it is improper to ride through the countryside alone with Sandy, and even though he is fully clothed underneath his armor, he feels that it is indecent to remove his armor in front of her.

One of the great ironies of the novel is found in Chapter 5. One of Hank Morgan's desires is to rid the country of superstitions. Yet, in order to gain control, he will use superstition to frighten the people into acknowledging his magical powers. Thus, Hank will use his practical Yankee knowledge of eclipses in order to perform his first miracle; the contrast between the practical and the miraculous is one of the comic devices which Twain uses throughout the novel.

CHAPTERS 6-8

Summary

Hank feels rather proud of himself and is almost impatient for the next day so that he can be "the center of all the nation's wonder and reverence." All such feelings vanish, however, when the men at arms come to get him, telling him that the stake is ready and that the execution has been moved up a day. Clarence joins him on the way to the courtyard and proudly announces that he is responsible for getting the king to change the date.

Hank is chained to the stake, and a monk begins to pray over him. Suddenly he stops, looking into the sky. Hank follows his gaze and notices that the eclipse has begun. He makes good use of the situation, telling those gathered that he will allow the darkness to proceed for a time. If the king agrees in good faith to make him the king's "perpetual minister and executive" and pay him one percent of any new revenues which he creates, Hank will allow the sun to shine again. The king agrees to the terms and orders Hank freed and clothed in rich clothing. Finally, when Hank notices that the eclipse is total and that the sun will soon peak beyond the moon, he says, "Let the enchantment dissolve and pass harmless away," much to the relief of those present.

In his new role as second in command to the king, Hank is given fine clothing and a choice suite in the castle. As he accustoms himself to his new quarters, he notices things that are lacking — bells, speaking tubes, chromo pictures, gas, candles, books, pens, paper, ink, glass, sugar, tea, coffee, tobacco, and many other things common to the nineteenth century.

In the meantime, the people of the kingdom are immensely interested in him. The eclipse frightened the whole kingdom, and everybody wants to see the magician who caused it. They flock in from all over the country to see him. It is clear that while they are there, they would like to see another miracle performed so they can carry the tale back to their villages.

The news that Merlin is busy spreading the idea that this "upstart" is a humbug causes Hank to decide that he will do something else. He has Merlin thrown into prison and then begins the preparations for having Merlin's tower blown to pieces by fire from heaven. Working with Clarence, he makes a great deal of blasting powder and constructs a lightning rod. They run wires from the lightning rod to caches of powder hidden throughout the tower. Then they wait until the weather is right.

At the first sign that there will be a storm, the event is announced to the people, and Hank has Merlin brought to him. He gives Merlin a chance to stop what is to take place, but Merlin cannot. So Hank, judging matters closely, waves his hand in the air three times, and the lightning strikes the lightning rod. There is a crash, fire spews forth, and the stones of the tower leap into the air. It is an effective miracle.

Hank, who is now known as The Boss, muses over the situation in which he finds himself. He has colossal power, and he plans to make some changes in the social and religious attitudes of the people so that they are more in line with what he thinks is right.

Commentary

After the great miracle, Hank could have demanded a title of nobility, but since he will later use all of his powers to destroy the concept of a privileged class of nobility, he refuses to ask for one; instead, he is extremely pleased with his newly invested title: he is *The Boss*, and known by this title, he will be admired and feared all over the kingdom. Ironically, The Boss wants to destroy the aristocracy, yet he fully enjoys the powers that he now has and plans to use them for his own advantages in the same way that the aristocracy uses their special privileges.

Furthermore, The Boss is filled with a need to be theatrical. Many of his actions are designed so as to bring a sense of applause to his own person; that is, he always seeks after the proper effect when he is performing a miracle. In Chapter 7, he makes sure that there are large numbers of people present to see his announced miracle of blowing up Merlin's castle. This act serves another purpose. In addition to bringing glory to The Boss, it discredits Merlin and, therefore, it allows The Boss to relax his guard.

In Chapter 8, Twain makes his first critique of the Roman Catholic Church. Later, he will continue his attacks on the Church in greater measure, but here he contents himself with commenting on how the Church has made common men into "worms"; thus, since the nation is composed largely of common men, the Church is responsible for making England "a nation of worms." He also questions here the duplicity of the church's helping to establish the concept about the "divinity of kings" and the "divine right of things." This only allows the aristocracy to treat the commoners in any way that the aristocracy so pleases. The Boss is determined to make the country into a republic where every man shall have an equal vote.

CHAPTERS 9 and 10

Summary

Tournaments are frequent events at Camelot, and The Boss usually attends them in order to see if there are any improvements that he can make. Indeed, he has such an interest in improvements that his first official act is to open a patent office. As this particular tournament takes place, he sets a priest in his Department of Public Morals and Agriculture to work toward learning to become a reporter, since he also wants to begin a newspaper.

During the course of the tournament, Sir Dinadan comes over and begins regaling The Boss with the same old jokes. This is cut short when Sir Dinadan is called out to fight Sir Gareth. Sir Gareth is giving him a good drubbing, and The Boss involuntarily says, "I hope to gracious he's killed!" Unfortunately, by the time he actually says these words, Sir Gareth has crashed into Sir Sagramor le Desirous, and Sir Sagramor thinks that the words were meant for him. He takes offense, and he names a date several years in the future—after he returns from searching for the Holy Grail—when he will demand satisfaction from The Boss.

In the four years following his fateful exclamation at the tournament, The Boss has the beginnings of nineteenth-century industrial civilization well underway in sixth-century England. His previous efforts have grown and spread. He has begun a military and a naval academy, and he has started stringing wires for both telegraphs and telephones, going across country and stringing the wires at night to avoid detection and to keep the Church from knowing what he is doing.

Indeed, in spite of all the changes which he has started, the country seems much the same as it was when he arrived in sixth-century

England. The main, obvious change is that revenues have quadrupled, while being spread about more equitably.

He can, therefore, take time out from his labors to undertake the quest that the king and many others think that he must undertake in order to honorably meet Sir Sagramor in the challenge match.

Commentary

In Chapters 9 and 10, The Boss has been in control for some undetermined length of time. Twain does not bother unduly with chronological details. At one tournament, Sir Sagramor, misunderstanding a comment, challenges The Boss to a duel; thus, throughout the novel, this duel is to be constantly remembered, and in Chapter 10, in order for The Boss to become "noble enough" to meet Sir Sagramor, he is encouraged to go on a quest. This prepares us for The Boss's first excursion into the rural parts of the kingdom.

CHAPTERS 11-15

Summary

People arrive in Camelot regularly with tales of captured princesses. These tales are accepted without question, and knights vie with one another for the honor of going out to "right the wrongs."

One day, a young lady with a tale about how her mistress and forty-four other "young and beautiful girls, pretty much all of them princesses," are held captive by "three stupendous brothers, each with four arms and one eye." King Arthur decides that this is *the* quest for The Boss—whether he wants it or not.

The Boss questions the young lady, whose name is Demoiselle Alisande la Carteloise. Finally, after confusing the girl and getting few answers that satisfy him, he gives up his questioning in disgust. He is appalled by the impropriety of this young woman's riding with him on his quest, but she *must* since she cannot give him any directions to follow.

Before The Boss leaves, he is given much good advice about how to handle himself, and, after a good breakfast, he is helped into his armor and carried out and set on his horse, things that he could not have managed himself.

The ride through the countryside is quite pleasant – until the sun has been up for several hours. The Boss begins to sweat, and he cannot get at his handkerchief to wipe the sweat away. Finally, he gives up, has Sandy (he has quickly given Alisande a nickname) take off his helmet, and lets her pour water into his suit of armor. But he now has a new problem: he cannot get back onto his horse by himself; therefore, they must wait until someone shows up who is willing to lift him up.

As night comes on, they find shelter from a storm. But still The Boss must keep his armor on because he can't take it off himself. In addition, he cannot ask Sandy to help him because having her help would make him feel as though he were undressing in public (even though he is well clothed inside the armor). He does not spend a good night, although his companion evidently does.

In the morning, they move on – Sandy on the horse and The Boss on foot – and before long, they come upon a group of freemen who are flattered by the idea that these two would want to share their food. As they eat, The Boss tries to stir up some sentiment for changing the form of government. For the most part, he gets no positive response of any kind, but one of the men does respond tentatively. The Boss thus writes a note to Clarence, and he sends this man to Camelot for training.

The Boss pays three pennies – an extravagant price – for his breakfast; the farmers then help him on his horse, and he and Sandy continue on their way. The next day, about mid-afternoon, they come across half a dozen knights, and Sandy fears that The Boss's life is in danger. The Boss, however, looks on this as an opportunity. He lights his pipe, and by the time that the knightly company has charged toward them, he has a good cloud of smoke coming through the bars of his helmet.

This breaks the charge, and the knights come to a halt several hundred yards away. The Boss is puzzled by this, until Sandy informs him that they are waiting to yield themselves to him. Sandy also takes care of the yielding, charging them "to appear at Arthur's court within two days and yield themselves, with horses and harnesses, and be my knights henceforth, and subject to my command." This impresses The Boss; he thinks that she handles it much better than *he* could have; his opinion of her is rising constantly.

As they ride on, The Boss asks Sandy about these knights. She tells him, at great length, all she knows. He, however, cannot follow the tales, and he falls asleep in the middle of Sandy's ramblings. He lectures Sandy about how to tell a story; she listens to him patiently, and then she goes on to tell the story her way.

As the day ends, Sandy's story is still unfinished, but they are approaching a large and impressive castle.

Commentary

One of Twain's most frequently used narrative techniques involves the innocent narrator taking a journey and encountering various adventures. In *Life on the Mississippi, Roughing It, Huck Finn, Innocents Abroad, The Prince and the Pauper*, and many other works, the concept of the narrator on a journey prevails. Here, we have the nineteenth-century Yankee traveling through sixth-century England, and his adventures are in the form of a series of contrasts. They are interesting reversals of Cervantes's *Don Quixote*, a novel that Twain greatly admired. In *Don Quixote*, the traveler was a knight who protected the innocent. Here, The Boss is a commoner who is *opposed* to knights. But one adventure is common to both stories: the story of the bewitched pigs is found in both works.

At first, when The Boss meets Sandy (Demoiselle Alisande la Carteloise), he is impatient with her, and he is also shocked that she will accompany him on his journey; it does not seem proper or decent for the two of them to travel together—alone. Thus, beginning with their meeting and their subsequent travels, we have a contrast between civilization and primitive innocence. In their first meeting, The Boss is professional, curt, businesslike, and skeptical. He wants written proof of her identity, a map, or directions to the so-called bewitched palace. He even calls her "innocent and idiotic" when she cannot understand why he would want all of the troublesome information that he is asking for, and she is incapable of understanding why he would even doubt her word. Therefore, until they are later married, The Boss continues to be patronizing and prudish; in contrast, Sandy is patient and loving.

In Chapter 12, when the two of them set out on their adventures, the contrast between the city and the lovely countryside is emphasized, especially in the opening paragraph where they "left the world behind and entered into the solemn great deeps and rich gloom of the forest. . . ." The quietness and peacefulness is reminiscent of Huck and Jim's trip down the Mississippi when no one is bothering them.

The irony is that in this lovely, peaceful solitude which The Boss so enjoys, he plans to start building huge, smoky factories filled with laboring people who must drudge through life. This is correlated by the fact that The Boss feels trapped in his suit of armor, and yet he would take these free and innocent people and trap them in the huge nineteenth-century factories – a trap much worse than the armor which he is now wearing.

The Boss's meeting with some "freemen" in Chapter 13 prompts some of his views on the Catholic Church and the ruling aristocracy. Here in Camelot, the majority of the people are ruled by only a half dozen people, and these people don't even seem to care because the Church has brainwashed them into believing that they are inferior and that they must be content with their place in life, a place assigned to them, according to the Church, by God Himself. Thus, they remain in servitude because of the alignment of the Church with the aristocracy.

CHAPTERS 16-18

Summary

Before The Boss and Sandy reach the castle, they come upon a knight who is wearing one of The Boss's signboards advertising soap. They chat for awhile, and this knight informs them that the castle belongs to Morgan le Fay, who is King Arthur's sister and King Uriens's wife.

The Boss encourages the knight, gives him a new advertising idea, and sends him on his way. Then they enter the castle and are taken before Morgan le Fay, her husband, and her son, Sir Uwaine le Blanchemains. While they are talking, a page trips and falls against her knee; she slips a knife into him without a thought and keeps on talking.

In the course of the conversation, The Boss forgets the relationship between the king and his sister and makes a complimentary remark about Arthur. Morgan le Fay orders them hauled to the dungeons, but the order is quickly withdrawn when Sandy informs her that this man is *The Boss*.

After prayers, they have dinner in a huge banquet hall, with over a hundred guests present. There is music, a great deal of food, and plentiful quantities of wine and mead.

About midnight, an old woman enters the hall and curses the queen for the murder of her grandson (the page whom the queen had stuck a knife into). The queen immediately orders her taken to the stake. Sandy, however, speaks for The Boss, telling Morgan le Fay to either cancel that order or The Boss will cause the castle to crumble around them. The queen cancels the order. So that she won't feel too humiliated, The Boss allows her to hang the musicians, who had played rather wretchedly.

The Boss would dearly love to go to bed, but Morgan le Fay insists that he must see her dungeons, especially the man who is on the rack. This man is accused of killing a deer on the royal preserves. The Boss tries to point out that an anonymous accusation is not proper, but le Fay will not accept that excuse. In the meantime, the man on the rack is tortured as they try to get him to confess. After watching for a moment, The Boss decides that the man must be turned loose, and Morgan concedes to The Boss's request.

As The Boss talks to the man, he learns – after word has been given that the man will not die – that the man did, indeed, kill the deer. He would not confess, however, because that would mean that his property would be confiscated, leaving his wife and child with nothing.

The Boss makes arrangements to send this man to Camelot for training and, afterward, sends him home. Then, because he did not like the executioner's actions, and because the priest had complained about him, The Boss makes the executioner the new leader of the new band that will play for the queen.

Before he and Sandy leave, The Boss asks to see the queen's dungeons. There, in small cells cut out of rock, are people, many of whom have been there so long that no one knows why they were put in the dungeons in the first place; indeed, the common practice in the kingdom is to throw them down there and forget about them.

The Boss orders forty-seven of the prisoners freed; the only person whom he leaves there is a lord who had killed a kinsman of Morgan le Fay.

Commentary

In earlier chapters, the knights have been seen as innocent and delightful children playing games and enjoying life. Now, however, when The Boss puts them between advertising sandwich-boards, they become truly ridiculous. The signs that the knights carry introduce another modern concept – advertising. This particular knight is advertising soap, and the advertising campaign is going so successfully that the workers in The Boss's soap factories are being overworked. Were we to be logical – a fallacy in reading a book such as this – we would have to point out that the advertising campaign could *not* work since no one except the clergy could read, thereby rendering the campaign unsuccessful. In fact, on this particular point, in Chapter 25 ("The Competitive Examination"), the young men who have been born of royal birth consider it an insult to be asked if they can read or write – that is a trivial task reserved for lowly clerks, and nobility should not be bothered by such trivia.

The entire idea of introducing both soap and advertising was done with the "several wholesome purposes in view toward the civilizing and uplifting of his nation." The irony here, as elsewhere, is that The Boss views civilization only in terms of material progress. This is one of the reasons that Twain refers to him as an "ignoramus."

In his meeting with Morgan le Fay, The Boss is again exposed to contradictory reactions in the same person. He has heard that she hates her brother, King Arthur, and that she is a vicious sorceress. Yet when he meets her, he is charmed by her "manner of pretty graces and graciousness." But when a page slips and falls upon her, she kills him with a dagger without a blink of an eye. From this act of atrocity, she immediately goes to her prayers. The Boss is mystified by this course of events, but he realizes that the Church has such a hold on the people that while the aristocracy can kill commoners at will, they must obey the call of the Church, which has the power to forgive them for their actions.

In Chapter 17, Twain is having some more of his good-natured fun. The Boss, after having freed the old grandmother, feels that Morgan le Fay needs someone to murder, so The Boss gives her permission to hang the band leader, the composer, and the entire band because they played so badly the night before. This is The Boss being arbitrarily cruel, and this is Mark Twain suggesting that bad artists who impose their bad art upon the public should be strung up; interestingly, later in the novel, when the press is prepared to publish books, Sir Dinadan publishes a book of his jokes, which is so bad that The Boss has him hanged because of the bad jokes.

In Chapter 18, Twain strikes out against the Church. Once The Boss is in total control, he will try to abolish the established Church—"my idea is to have it [religion] cut up into forty free sects, so that they will police each other, as had been the case in the United States in my time. Concentration of power in a political machine; it was invented for that; it is nursed, cradled, preserved for that; it is an enemy to human liberty." In this regard, one should note that many great writers and thinkers have seen a strong centralized church as being more of a political force than a spiritual force. Significantly, later in the novel, the Church *does* assert its political strength, and it proves to be more effective than The Boss's scientific realism.

Also in Chapter 18, Twain reiterates an idea that was the basis of an earlier novel, *The Prince and the Pauper*. In that novel, the prince and the pauper exchange clothes and no one can tell which is the prince and which is the pauper—except by the clothes which they wear. In this chapter, a man was imprisoned for saying that he believed that "if you were to strip the nation naked and send a stranger through the crowd, he couldn't tell the king from a quack doctor, nor a duke from a hotel clerk." Later on, we will see a verification of this idea when the king dresses as a peasant and goes unrecognized among his people.

CHAPTERS 19 and 20

Summary

The next morning, The Boss and Sandy take to the road again, and Sandy begins once more her tale of the knights, the story that she left unfinished when they reached Morgan le Fay's castle.

After they cover about ten miles in three hours, they stop for a long lunchbreak. While they are there, Sir Madok de la Montaine, another of The Boss's advertising knights, comes upon them. He is cursing and swearing, for another knight has played a practical joke on him, sending him across fields and through swamps for a chance to sell his wares to five of the people whom The Boss just released from Morgan le Fay's dungeons. He vows that he will avenge this insult.

Toward noon, two days later, Sandy informs The Boss that they are approaching an ogre's castle. When she points it out to him, all he can see is a pigsty filled with pigs. Finally, to keep her happy – she is sure that it is a castle and that the pigs are princesses – he tells her that it must be enchanted to his sight, but he agrees to "rescue" the princesses. He does so by buying the pigs from the three swineherds, paying more than the market value. Then they drive the pigs to a castle about ten miles farther on. They have a great deal of difficulty keeping the "princesses" together, and when they arrive at the castle, servants have to be sent out to find several of the "princesses."

Commentary

Sandy's story in Chapter 19 does very little for the novel except slow it down and bore the reader. Twain's editor would have done well to have cut this chapter severely.

In Chapter 20, focusing on the rescue of the princesses who have been turned into pigs by some evil sorcerer or sorceress, we have a scene that is evocative of scenes from Cervantes's novel, where Don Quixote will often be blinded and see things from a different reality than other people do. In a reverse sort of way, The Boss *pretends* that his sight is bad, and to pacify Sandy, he pretends that he sees things as she does. But whereas Don Quixote was a madman and an idealist in a nation of sane people, The Boss is a sane man of practicality in a nation of fools and children.

CHAPTERS 21-23

Summary

The next day, The Boss and Sandy leave the pigs in the castle – whose it is they never discover – and they set out again. Shortly thereafter, they meet a band of pilgrims who are headed toward the Valley of Holiness – a place where the holiness of the monks and the prayers of a holy abbot once brought forth a stream of water in a desert. Some time later, the monks persuaded the abbot to build a bath, and they bathed in it; this caused the well to dry up. Once the bath was destroyed, however, the stream sprang forth again.

In the afternoon, The Boss and Sandy overtake another, less cheerful group, a procession of slaves being herded by a slavemaster who goads them along with his whip. The Boss would like to free them all immediately, but he feels that he cannot change things too quickly.

The following morning, they meet another of the salesmen-knights, who tells them that business has been fine and that the well at the Valley of Holiness has dried up again. The monks have sent to Camelot to see if The Boss would come; if he could not, Merlin was invited. Merlin has been there for three days, working on the problem. On hearing this news, The Boss writes an order for materials and assistance, and he sends this knight off to Camelot, urging him to go swiftly. He plans to continue on to the Valley of Holiness.

The Boss and Sandy reach the monastery by nightfall, and the abbot rejoices that The Boss has come. Indeed, the abbot urges him to begin work immediately, but The Boss demurs, saying that it would not be right for him to do anything until Merlin has admitted defeat. Yet, even though The Boss will not take charge, the monastery is much cheered by his arrival, and for the first time in the week and a half since the well dried up, there is a good deal of food and drink and merriment that night.

The next day, The Boss examines the fountain, which is an ordinary well, dug and walled up in the ordinary way. He suspects that the well has sprung a leak; so he has the monks lower him into the well; there, he finds a huge hole in the wall of the well, and he begins to plan his campaign to restore the well. His first point is to suggest how difficult it will be to do so; it is good for business.

He talks with Sandy about the hermits, and afterward, they visit the various hermits during the afternoon. One of them rapidly bows to his feet almost continuously; later, The Boss uses him to supply the power to run a sewing machine that produces shirts.

About noon on Saturday, Merlin makes his last great effort. When that fails, he predicts that no one will *ever* be able to make the fountain flow again. The abbot is most upset, but The Boss suggests that there is still a chance that he might be able to do something.

That evening, the two men sent by Clarence in response to The Boss's request arrive with the equipment which The Boss needs—

"tools, pump, lead pipe, Greek fire, sheaves of big rockets, Roman candles, colored fire sprays, electric apparatus, and a lot of sundries." Toward midnight, after a nap, they go out to the well, and by sunrise they have the well repaired and everything in place for the miracle. By noon, the water in the well has risen to its customary level. They build a platform, arrange the Greek fire at the corners, prepare the rockets, and fence off the area around the platform.

The performance begins at 10:30 with the arrival of the abbot's procession; masses of people have come to see what will happen. Finally, The Boss stands up and begins to pronounce long, strange words in German, lighting a Greek fire at the end of each name. Finally, he pronounces the name of the spirit that has shut off the water supply and sets off the hogshead of rockets. By the glare of the rockets, the crowd sees the water gushing forth from the chapel.

Commentary

In Chapter 21, The Boss meets a group of pilgrims, and he is surprised to see that the procession includes people from all occupations, professions, and social ranks. Twain is obviously echoing here the pilgrims of Chaucer's famous *Canterbury Tales.* In this tale, the only way that people of different social classes and different occupations could be found in each other's company was by their making a religious pilgrimage. Also, Chaucer's group of pilgrims were very much like these pilgrims; that is, they are a "pleasant, friendly, sociable herd; pious, happy, merry, and full of unconscious coarseness and innocent indecencies." The prude in the Yankee emerges, and he is offended by the vulgarity which he hears. The description of the pilgrims, then, continues Twain's double vision of the people of this country – innocent, yet indecent by nineteenth-century standards.

In contrast to the pilgrims, the treatment of the group of slaves anticipates Chapter 34, where The Boss and King Arthur will be captured and made slaves themselves. Thus, here, while The Boss wants to do away with slavery, the abolition must wait until King Arthur himself has felt the yoke of slavery.

While religion often comes under criticism in this novel, the most sustained criticism on religion occurs in these chapters, during The Boss's visit to the Valley of Holiness. In other parts of the novel, Twain constantly attacks the authoritarianism of the Roman Catholic

Church, but here, his views are more concentrated; he sees the Church as being undemocratic, despotic, and absolutist. He also sees it as being hypocritical in its complete support of the aristocracy. Furthermore, the Church even aids the nobility in pillaging from the peasants and other commoners, but mainly, it fosters ignorance and superstitions. At the end of the novel, the Church is able to play upon the superstitions of the people in Chapter 41 ("Interdict") in order to regain control of the country and to eject The Boss from his position of authority.

The first aspect to come under attack is the absurdity found in making a pilgrimage to worship hermits, many of whom will ultimately become saints. For Twain, a hermit (and also a saint) is, by definition, an abnormal person—a weirdo. That people would come and worship such strange, bizarre people is totally confusing to The Boss. The rationale behind worshipping someone who lives on nuts and berries and goes naked is beyond his Yankee common sense. Living the life of a hermit—that is, living in pure asceticism—contributes nothing to material progress or to the betterment of humanity, and rather than being worshipped, these strange creatures should be ridiculed. Thus, to illustrate his denunciation of this type of asceticism, The Boss is extremely critical of the hermit who sits on a pillar sixty feet high and spends the entire day "bowing his body ceaselessly and rapidly almost to his feet." Because of his large pillar, this hermit will later be known as St. Stylite. The practical Connecticut Yankee sees this movement as being wasted power; thus, he creates a method of attaching a power take-off to the hermit which will, by his incessant motions, create enough power to run a sewing machine which will, in turn, produce *"genuine St. Stylite"* shirts. At least something practical is attained because of the hermit's useless, and heretofore non-productive, bowing. Other hermits are shown doing equally useless things, and yet being worshipped for doing them.

Twain also pokes good-natured fun by some sly or indecent observations—such as the monastery being on one hill and the nunnery (or convent) on the other hill, and in between the two lies the home for foundlings, implying that the latter place is filled with the children of the monks and nuns.

The Boss's desire for theatricality is shown again in the miracle which he performs in the Valley of Holiness. After he has used his

Yankee practicality to patch up the hole in the well, he then has hordes of people gather for the "miracle," which is accompanied by "Greek fires" and "Roman candles"—names given to fireworks, but, one should note, *pagan* names used to celebrate a Christian miracle. The people are awed, and The Boss, greatly to his satisfaction, is elevated in the sight of everyone present. Ironically, The Boss has once again used superstition to gain control over superstitious people whom he wants to educate *not* to be superstitious.

CHAPTERS 24-26

Summary

After this miracle, The Boss's reputation is great in the Valley of Holiness, so he decides to suggest that a bath be built. He assures the abbot that it will not dry up the water again and that an error had been made the previous time, when it was believed that the bath had been the cause of the fountain's failure. The abbot agrees, and when the bath is finished, he is the first to try it out.

A heavy cold and a touch of rheumatism ensue and leave The Boss weak. Later, while walking about the valley to get his strength back, he discovers a cave that had been abandoned by a hermit. He looks inside and finds one of his telephone linemen putting in a phone. He uses the opportunity to call Clarence and find out what is happening back in Camelot. One thing that he learns is that the king and the queen, with a large party of nobles, have just set out toward the Valley of Holiness. He also learns that the king has started raising a standing army, one of his suggestions to the king, although he had wanted to oversee its development.

When he returns to the monastery, another magician has arrived; his specialty is announcing what great people around the globe are doing. The Boss tests him by asking what Arthur is doing; the new magician says that Arthur is presently asleep, but that the next day, Arthur and the court will ride to the north—away from the Valley of Holiness—for two days. The Boss contradicts him, telling him that the king and his party will be in this very valley by evening two days hence.

The new magician, however, seems to sway the crowd, for they make no preparations for the king's arrival. Thus, The Boss uses the

telephone to check on the king's progress and manages to gather together something of a crowd to go out and greet the king. When the
abbot and the monks discover that Arthur is indeed arriving, they
dash out to greet him, although they take the time to–in Twain's
words–ride the rival magician out on a rail.

In Chapter 25, we see that King Arthur always takes care of business matters wherever he is. The Commission charged with examining
candidates for posts in the army arrives with the king, and the examination of officer candidates takes place. The Commission and the king in-
sist that the main qualifications that an officer must have is a noble
lineage that extends at least four generations into the past. Thus, The
Boss's candidate, who has been trained at his "West Point," is denied a
post, even though The Boss leads him through a series of questions that
shows that he does know military matters thoroughly. Another candidate is given a post because he has the requisite lineage, even though
The Boss shows that he knows *nothing* about military matters.

Later, The Boss proposes to the king that he form a regiment to
be considered the king's own, formed of officers only, that can do as
it pleases during battles. The other regiments would have to follow
orders and do the dirty work of fighting.

In Chapter 26, we learn that The Boss is planning to go about the
countryside as a "petty freeman" in order to find out what things are
like on that level of society. When he tells the king about his plan,
Arthur decides that he will come along.

In the meantime, however, the king must take care of "the king's
evil business," a time when all those who are genuinely ill (they are
screened) can come forward, touch the king, and receive a small piece
of gold–or, now, one of The Boss's new nickles. In this process, many
are cured because of their faith that they will be cured.

It is a long and tedious process, but the tedium is relieved by the
sound of a boy's hawking the first edition of the Camelot *Weekly
Hosannah and Literary Volcano*. The Boss gets a copy through the
window and spends his time looking through it rather critically. His
judgment, however, is that it is a pretty fair first effort, although he
sees some things which he wants changed. It is passed about from
hand to hand, and the people are amazed.

Commentary

In Chapter 24, The Boss again uses his Yankee ingenuity and
practicality to discredit another magician. By the use of the tele-

phone wire that he finds in a hermit's cave during one of his walks, he finds out from Clarence that King Arthur and his court are on the way to the Valley of Holiness. Thus, when the rival magician has everyone entranced by his ability to tell what people in faraway places are doing at any given moment, The Boss, who *does* know what Arthur is doing, uses this information to trap the charlatan. Once again, however, The Boss is playing upon the superstitions of the people while also asserting that he is trying to educate the people *not* to be superstitious. Ironically, none of these simple people can see through the hoax of the rival magician; they reject him only when The Boss's prediction comes true; they are truly a fickle group, ready to quickly change their allegiances. Thus, at the end, all of The Boss's teachings will be lost on everyone except those whom he has trained since birth.

In Chapter 25, Twain is able to make further comments on the injustices caused by the Church and its collaboration with the aristocracy. This is shown in the scene where the young girl loses all of her property to the bishop (also a member of the nobility) because of *le droit du seigneur* (the rights due to the lord of the manor).

Furthermore, The Boss thinks that ability, talent, and intelligence should be the key qualities in choosing commissioned officers to defend the country. Thus, he is totally depressed and defeated when he discovers that lineage is more important than intelligence and ability. As a result, the defense of the country will lie in the hands of the nobility simply because they *are* nobility – not because they are capable of defending the country.

Twain uses this episode to bring his narrative to a halt and to offer his own personal polemic on royalty and democracy. In one of his most famous statements, he writes: "Men write many fine and plausible arguments in support of monarchy, but the fact remains that where every man in a state has a vote, brutal laws are impossible." The Boss also feels that the people in this kingdom have been debased so long by the brutality of the monarchy that they are poor material for a democracy. Furthermore, he believes that the masterminds of history who have moved civilization forward have come from its masses – "not from its privileged class"; therefore, the following is a self-proven fact: "even the best governed and most free and most enlightened monarchy is still behind the best conditions attainable by its people." These thoughts of The Boss, spoken here in a polemic digression, do not always coincide with the depiction of the characters of Camelot. The individual person, such as King Arthur, is depicted as being a royal man of good character and fine appearance. Thus, Twain has his double focus—in his polemics, he attacks certain institutions, but in his narrative, he depicts aspects of these institutions or individuals as being fine and noble.

Chapter 26 does very little to move the plot forward except to let us know that The Boss announces his intention to tour England as a common peasant. Additionally, The Boss's first newspaper is presented to us, and the comedy of this newspaper lies in how crudely it is printed, but no one can read it anyway, and it is passed around merely as a curiosity piece.

CHAPTERS 27-30

Summary

Late that night, The Boss cuts the king's hair, trims his beard, and dresses him in a long robe and sandals. In this costume, they can pass as poor freemen, and they slip away from the monastery just before dawn.

The first problem occurs when some of the nobility pass by; the king is not ready to take the humble attitude that is necessary, and he does not do a very good job of it. Fortunately, his behavior elicits nothing more than scowls.

The next day, the king produces a dirk (a dagger), which he bought from a smuggler at the inn where they had stayed; it is illegal for members of the lower class to possess such weapons, and The Boss must talk quickly to persuade the king to throw the dirk away.

As they walk along, the king is perplexed that The Boss does not know what, in particular, will happen tomorrow. The Boss must explain that his special kind of prophecy is the kind that can more easily see 1300 years into the future than it can see into the next day; the king is satisfied with this explanation.

In the meantime, every time a knight passes by, The Boss must restrain the king, for the sight fires the king's martial spirit. During one such encounter, The Boss takes a stroke of a whip that is meant for the king, and at another, he has to use a bomb to save them from the charge of a group of knights whom the king challenges.

By the morning of the fourth day, The Boss has decided that the king must be drilled in "proper behavior" so that he will not disclose his true identity when they meet people or when they enter a dwelling. First, The Boss discusses the way the king walks, how he stands, and how he looks at people, plus the way he talks, addresses people, and how he treats his companion – in effect, The Boss tries to remold the king's entire pattern of behavior. He also tries to tell the king something about the life of the people who they are pretending to be, but this means little or nothing to the king, since it is not at all like life as *he* has experienced it. Although they work long and hard at remaking the king's new "image," and although the king gains some ability to approximate the appropriate actions, he never truly succeeds because he cannot understand the spiritual state of the lower classes.

In the middle of the afternoon, they arrive at a hut that seems deserted. They enter it cautiously, finding a woman on the floor. She tells them to go quickly, since this place is cursed by God and by the Church. They decide to care for the woman, and here, the king takes an active part, even though the woman is suffering from smallpox. Her husband is dead, as is one of her daughters. The king brings the remaining daughter down from the loft, and she dies in her mother's arms. The Boss and the king learn that this family had a good life, more or less, until this year. Then their sons were arrested for a crime that they hurried to report. As a result, the harvesting of the family's crop suffered, and they were fined for not providing the full complement of workers for harvesting their lord's crops. In addition, the Church condemned them because the woman spoke blasphemous words under the pressures which she suffered. Now, she can only wait and hope to die.

By midnight, the woman is dead. As the king and The Boss leave the hut, they hear voices, and they quickly conceal themselves, learning that it is the three sons who have come home.

The king finally figures out that these boys have escaped, and he feels that he must do something about recapturing them. The Boss, of course, has entirely different feelings about the matter, and he works hard to convince the king to forget about it.

Only the fact that they see a fire in the distance is turning the king's thoughts to other matters. The Boss and continue to move through the forest, and they come across a hanging from a tree, and then they discover two other bodies. In the space of the next mile, they discover six more bodies dangling from branches.

Finally, they come upon a house and manage to convince the woman that they are travelers who have lost their way during the night and are badly in need of hospitality. She gives them a place to sleep and feeds them when they awaken late in the afternoon. While they eat, she tells them that the manor house of Abblasoure has been burned and the master killed. Men have been out all night hunting the men who, it is thought, are responsible for this crime.

The king announces that he has seen three possible suspects; he is sure that his hosts will be eager to go out and spread the news. The Boss then notices some concern on the faces of the couple, so he volunteers to go out with the charcoal burner in whose house they have rested. Questioning the man, The Boss realizes the possibility that the charcoal burner is related, in some way, to these young men and the burning of the manor house. He also learns that no one in the community would want to see them hanged; indeed, he learns that the man of the house had no desire to be out the night before and went out only because staying home would have been considered suspicious. For himself, he is happy that the lord got his just deserts.

Commentary

In Chapters 27 through 30, we have a large segment of the novel dealing with the wanderings of King Arthur and The Boss, dressed as peasants and encountering various adventures, most of which are created so as to show King Arthur how much injustice prevails throughout his kingdom.

In Chapter 27, The Boss tries to make the king look like a peasant by dressing him in peasant's clothes and cutting his hair in the same manner as that of a peasant. As Twain often advocated, it is the dress that often makes the man; undress two people and you cannot tell the royal one from the plain one. Here, we have Twain's double focus again. In Twain's polemic, we have his views about dress stated overtly, but when The Boss tries to make the king act like a peasant, the king's nobility cannot be concealed. Thus, we have the contrast between Twain's view and Twain's presentation.

Chapter 28 continues to emphasize the fact that the king has such a royal bearing that he must be drilled again and again to overcome this fact. The main trouble is that the king cannot mentally understand the sufferings and the "spiritlessness" of the lower classes.

The purpose of Chapter 29 is to show the basic humanity of the king. In spite of the threat to his own life—he might catch smallpox and die himself—the king is nevertheless determined to help the poor suffering woman even though she ironically blames her present problems on the Church and the king, totally unaware that the complaint is made to the king himself.

In Chapter 30, even though King Arthur knows that the old woman's sons are innocent, yet the mere fact that they have escaped from the dungeon of one of the nobility means that they have to capture the innocent men and return them to the nobility for punishment. The Boss is again mystified concerning the amount of loyalty that there is to other members of the royalty. The nobility was able "to imprison these men, without proof, and starve their kindred, [and it] was not harm, for they were merely peasants and subject to the will and pleasure of their lord . . . but for these [innocent] men to break out of unjust captivity was insult and outrage."

When The Boss goes out with the charcoal burner, he discovers that the man *had* to participate in a hunt for his friends or else he would be under suspicion himself. Yet even he is glad that the evil lord is dead. This prompts Twain to assert again the value of the common man for "a man *is* a man. . . . Whole ages of abuse and oppression cannot crush the manhood clear out of him. . . ." Then The Boss decides that this is the type of material that he will use when he gradually establishes his republic.

CHAPTERS 31-34

Summary

After this confession has been made and The Boss accepts it completely, the two men walk toward the hamlet, talking. In the village, The Boss makes the acquaintance of a number of people and learns what he can about the matter of wages here. One of the things that he discovers is that the new coins which he introduced are being used widely.

As they talk to various people, The Boss invites a number of them to come to Marco's (the charcoal burner) on Sunday for dinner. Lest Marco become too upset, he insists that he will pay for the whole thing, and he makes a lavish provision for the dinner. He also has Marco buy new clothing for himself and his wife, saying that it is a gift from Jones (the king), who is too shy to say anything himself.

Sunday is a beautiful day, and the guests arrive at the Marco's about noon. They gather under a huge tree outside and spend a good deal of time talking and becoming better acquainted. Dowley, the blacksmith, has been doing well, and he is in an expansive mood, telling about how he has worked his way up in the world and how he can now afford to give his family such luxuries as fresh meat on the table twice a month and salt meat eight times more.

About this time, as The Boss had planned, the Marcos bring out a number of chairs, some other furniture, and a great variety of provisions. In addition, the storekeeper's son arrives with the bill, which The Boss treats casually, even though it seems like a horrible sum to all those present. He pays it easily, and the blacksmith is crushed by this show of wealth.

The Boss now thinks that he has these men at a psychological advantage, so he begins a discussion about wages and buying power. He tries to get them to see that wages are important only in relationship to what can be bought with those wages, that a man with high wages and a man with low wages are equally well off if they can both buy the same amount of goods with what they earn. He fails totally.

Then, partly out of frustration at his failure to make these people see his point, he turns to the idea of a freeman being able to work where he wishes, for the wages he chooses. In his efforts to make a point against Dowley, the blacksmith, his comments suggest that he could now turn Dowley in for violating the law; very suddenly, all the people at the gathering are very quiet and suspicious. Thus, he tries to win back their trust and to show them that they have nothing to fear from him. At that moment, however, the king rejoins them after his nap and begins talking about agriculture. He quickly convinces the men that he is crazy, and they charge them. The Boss and the king have the better of the fight, but The Boss soon realizes that their hosts have left, undoubtedly to fetch help.

As they are chased, they throw the pursuers off their trail, and they use a stream to cover their tracks and then climb a tree, using a bough that was hanging over the water. They are, however, found when one of their pursuers climbs the tree by mistake. Yet they still manage to hold out until they are smoked out of their tree. When they land on the ground, they are immediately set upon, and a fight ensues.

They are "apparently rescued" when a gentleman and his retinue come upon the scene. They are given horses, fed, and housed at an inn, and told to ride ahead to the next town, where they will be safe. When they arrive, they come across a troop of slaves which The Boss had first seen on his way to the Valley of Holiness. They soon become a part of this band of slaves, however, for Lord Grip, their apparent rescuer, has them bound and sold. Although the king rages, it makes no difference.

Commentary

Chapters 31 and 32 are interludes which have nothing or very little to do with the plot. That is, the supposed purpose of this section is to expose the king to the customs of his subjects, but these chapters neither move the plot forward, nor do they serve to inform the king about his subjects.

The most amusing thing about the chapters is the manner in which The Boss wants to play the bountiful host and impress these rather lowly people. No matter how much power, he has, The Boss still wants to be theatrical and attract attention to himself. Of course, it is also human nature to want to put a braggart in his place, as The Boss does with Dowley, who brags about having meat twice a month and having all sorts of luxuries just before the Marcos bring out the plentiful bounty that The Boss has provided.

In Chapter 33, which again does not move the plot forward and thus is another digression, we see The Boss attempting to explain the economic theory that wages are important only in so far as what they will buy. He is a complete failure at this, and resenting the fact that the peasants don't see his point, he childishly begins to get revenge on them.

In order to show them how illogical they are, he creates another analogy about the absurdity of the pillory, and at the end of this analogy, he has placed all of the peasants in a position of being placed in the pillory. Rather than making a logical point, The Boss has only turned the peasants against him, and thus, at the first opportunity, they will use their fear to betray him.

In Chapter 34, this opportunity soon presents itself. When King Arthur makes his absurd remarks concerning agriculture, the superstitious men are going to use this opportunity to seize the "mad man" and "the one [who] would betray us." All these events are leading up to the enslavement of The Boss and the king. The comedy of the situation is that The Boss brings a higher price than the king does at the slave market, and both men are annoyed that they are sold for so little, for they both believe that they should have brought a far higher price. Since King Arthur cannot prove himself to be a freeman, and he and The Boss are sold into slavery, they find themselves upon the slave block; thus, Twain hopes that everyone will realize the "hellish" horror of slavery. The king's enslavement will, however, cause him later to abolish the entire concept of slavery.

CHAPTERS 35-38

Summary

The king is upset that the price he brought was only seven dollars, and he complains incessantly. In point of fact, his style of conduct is at odds with his apparent condition, and this discrepancy is responsible for his low price and for the fact that he becomes a difficult slave to sell. Yet, despite even the conditions of his tramping around the country and of being beaten regularly (even the king's body is battered), nothing seems to reduce his spirits.

At one point in their travels, The Boss and the king are caught in a snowstorm, and although the slave master keeps them going to keep warm, they are nearly exhausted. At this point, a woman runs up to them, begging for protection from the pursuing mob, which wants to burn her. The slave master turns her over to them, then he gathers the troops of slaves around the fire to keep them warm and protect his investment.

Finally, they reach London. There, they see a young woman about to be put to death for stealing a small piece of cloth so that she might sell it and thus be able to feed her baby daughter. She has been reduced to these circumstances because her husband had been impressed as a sailor, and she knew nothing about it. Before she is hanged, a priest speaks forcefully about the injustice of the situation, and he promises her that her child will be cared for.

In London, The Boss spots newspaper boys, so he knows that Clarence is working swiftly. He also notices that wires for either the telephone or the telegraph have been strung in the city; thus, he begins making plans to escape. At first, these plans are quite extravagant, particularly in the matter of what he will do to the slave master.

The opportunity for escape arrives when a man comes for a third time to haggle about the price of The Boss. This man's outer garment is fastened in the front with a metal contraption containing a long pin, and as he bargains with the slave master, The Boss manages to loosen one of these clasps. Using this pin as a lock pick, he frees himself. Just as he is about to free the king, however, the slave master comes in. Yet he does not notice anything unusual, and so he leaves. At this point, the king urges The Boss to fetch the slave master back. He dashes out and tackles the figure whom he sees retreating from the building, and a fierce scuffle ensues. This brings the watchmen, and they take the two combatants into custody; only then does The Boss discover that he tackled the wrong man.

When he is taken to court the next morning, The Boss relates a tale about being a slave belonging to Earl Grip, who had been sent into London to fetch a physician when the Earl became suddenly ill; he had been running as fast as he could when he happened to run into this man, who seized him by the throat and began beating him. The Boss is quickly released, and he returns to the slave quarters and finds them all gone. He learns that the slaves had revolted in the night and had killed the slave master. All the slaves have been condemned to die in the next day or so.

The Boss quickly buys some new clothing and arranges a disguise of sorts. Then he finds the telephone office, where he forces the attendant to put in a call to Camelot and to ask for Clarence. After a time, Clarence is reached. They decide that a mighty force of knights will be the best way to handle the situation; Clarence assures him that they will leave in half an hour.

After he leaves the telephone office, The Boss decides to try and make contact with people he knows. However, he is over-confident and walks, literally, into the shackles of the law and is put into prison with the other slaves. There, he learns that they are to be hanged in the middle of that afternoon, before the knights can get from Camelot to London.

About four in the afternoon, the slaves are taken out to be hanged; it is a superb day. The king creates a diversion when he leaps up and proclaims himself to be Arthur, King of Britain. Of course, the crowd does not believe a word he says; instead, they are amused, and they call for him to speak, but he will not.

Three slaves are hanged in short order, and the blindfold is then put on the king. Suddenly, five hundred knights in mail come riding up on *bicycles*, led by Sir Launcelot. The knights swarm upon the scaffold, tossing the sheriffs and others off, and freeing the king and The Boss. Clarence has also come along, and he explains how he has had the knights drilling for a long time; they have just been waiting for a chance to show off their newly acquired skills.

Commentary

Again in Chapter 35, we are given Twain's double focus. Even though Twain says that only clothes can determine royalty from nobility, yet The Boss is constantly impressed with the spirit and bearing of the king because no amount of slavery or abuse can break his royal spirit.

Even though there is the implication that The Boss could arrange for their freedom, he deliberately chooses to keep the king in slavery until the king realizes the horrors of slavery; then, hopefully, he will, of his own accord, want to abolish it. In addition, even though The Boss is indignant and horrified by the various injustices that he has encountered so far, King Arthur has shown no particular concern for the various injustices and cruelties that they have encountered, and it is not until they are both made slaves that King Arthur personally feels the marks of injustice and vows to abolish at least that social crime from his realm.

Chapter 35 also shows Twain's penchant to sink suddenly into the most maudlin bathos. In this chapter, for example, we witness the burning of a woman at the stake during a snowstorm with her two daughters clinging to her and slaves being forced to gather around her to absorb the warmth from her burning body in order to keep from perishing of the bitter cold; in addition, Twain includes a scene in which a young nursing mother is hanged for stealing a small bit of cloth. The late nineteenth-century reading public, one should remember, was the same public that adored attending melodramas at the theater, but today when we make fun of the typical nineteenth-century "mellerdrammer," we also find such scenes as the above to be almost embarrassingly sentimental. More important, however, in these events, we are not told how the king responds to them, or if they have any effect at all upon him.

In Chapter 36, we see that The Boss could have escaped earlier, but he waited until the king had recanted his position concerning slavery; then The Boss merely uses his Yankee ingenuity to pick the locks, and no one is smart enough to understand how he did it.

In Chapter 37, King Arthur is exposed to the dreadful conditions of English prisons, but we still do not know what effect it has upon him. The change in the time of the death sentence parallels the change in The Boss's death sentence at the beginning of the novel when the eclipse appeared a day earlier. Thus, in terms of plot, we await now to see how Twain handles this change. Actually, Twain's handling of this episode is a type of the cheapest melodrama to be found in first-class literature. In the use of the knights' being dressed in armor and riding to the rescue on bicycles, the readers' plausibility is stretched outlandishly, and the entire execution is handled in such a slipshod fashion that it has no place in an otherwise serious book. If one did not know Twain's penchant for the melodramatic atmosphere and for the sentimental effect, one could almost make out a case that he was satirizing works of melodrama, but unfortunately, Twain did not make such fine distinctions.

CHAPTER 39 and the FINAL P.S. BY M. T.

Summary

Just a few days after his return to Camelot, The Boss must fight Sir Sagramor le Desirous to give satisfaction for the supposed malediction several years earlier. In this tournament, a new rule takes effect: each combatant can use any weapon which he chooses.

Merlin, of course, is on the side of Sir Sagramor, working to make him invisible to his opponent although visible to everyone else. Indeed, all of the knights are siding with Sir Sagramor, since The Boss has made known his anti-knighthood feelings. He is alone with his servants at his end of the field.

The two combatants meet in front of the king's stand. Sir Sagramor is in full battle regalia and is seated upon a huge, magnificent horse. The Boss is in tights and riding a medium-sized, quick horse.

The tournament begins, and the two opponents charge at each other. The Boss uses the agility of his horse to evade Sir Sagramor's lance; he does this several times, until Sir Sagramor loses his temper, and the fight turns into a game of tag. Finally, The Boss takes out a lasso; he ropes Sir Sagramor and yanks him from his saddle.

Several other knights challenge The Boss, as is their right, and each of them, including Sir Launcelot, meets the same fate. After this bout, however, Merlin manages to steal the lasso. When the bugle is blown again for yet another joust, Sir Sagramor rides out, and The Boss pretends to find him by the sound of his horse's hooves. Sir Sagramor tells The Boss that he is a dead man and that The Boss will die on Sir Sagramor's sword. When the king suggests that The Boss borrow a weapon to replace the missing rope, Sir Sagramor denies him this right.

Sir Sagramor charges, but The Boss remains unmoving. When Sir Sagramor is some fifteen paces away, The Boss pulls out a pistol, which he has made, and he shoots Sir Sagramor, killing him. The crowd is amazed, for there is no apparent reason for the man to be dead. No one else steps forward to challenge The Boss, so he challenges them all. Five hundred knights mount and charge, and when they get close enough, The Boss pulls out both of his guns and begins to shoot; nine knights fall—and then, suddenly the others stop, they stare, and they turn in flight.

In the ensuing three years, The Boss reveals the mines and factories and workshops that he had started but had kept hidden. He also continues to challenge any and all knights who wish to face him—alone or *en masse*. He has no takers.

Many changes have taken place in these three years. Books begin to be printed, railroads begin running, and steam and electricity become available throughout the country; machines that run on these modes of power have been introduced, telephones and tele-graph lines are everywhere, steamboats are plying the Thames, and a navy has been formed. The Boss is ready to try to overthrow the Catholic Church and to introduce universal suffrage.

The Boss has also married Sandy, and they have a child – a daughter – named Hello-Central. Just as things are going entirely his way, however, The Boss's daughter, Hello-Central, becomes very ill. The Boss decides to halt all of his plans of progress in order to take care of her, and when the doctors suggest that sea air is necessary to bring her back to health, he takes a man-of-war and a party of two-hundred and sixty men and goes cruising. After two weeks of sailing, they land on the French coast, decide to stay for awhile, and send the ship back for supplies.

Shortly after the ship has sailed, Hello-Central takes a turn for the worse, and The Boss's attention is taken up with caring for her. One should note here that The Boss married Sandy for the sake of ap-pearance. She, however, turned out to be a fine wife and an excellent mother. She chose the name "Hello-Central" because The Boss cried it out in his dreams (his girlfriend back in Hartford had been a tele-phone operator); Sandy, of course, thought it was the name of a lost girlfriend.

After two and a half weeks, Hello-Central recovers, but the ship, which was supposed to be gone only three or four days, has not re-turned. After another two weeks without a ship, The Boss returns to England to find out what has happened. When he arrives, everything is shut down. The Church has struck back; an Interdict is in effect.

In disguise, The Boss sets out for Camelot alone. When he reaches it, the gate is wide open, and everything is silent. The Boss finds Clarence alone in his quarters, and the electric lights have been replaced by rag lamps. The whole business, Clarence tells The Boss, was caused by Launcelot and Guenever. Launcelot manipulated the stock market to undo a number of knights, including Sir Agravane and Sir Mordred, nephews of the king. As a result, twelve knights laid an ambush for Launcelot, but he killed all but Mordred. As a result of this, the country became divided; some supported the king in his grievance, while others supported Sir Launcelot.

Then the king proposed to purify the queen by fire, but Launce-lot and his men came to the rescue. This, of course, intensified the lines of battle. A truce between the parties was arranged, except for

Sir Gawaine, whose brothers had been slain in the fighting. He told Launcelot to expect an attack. Launcelot left for another stronghold, and Gawaine followed, luring the king with him. Unfortunately, Arthur left Mordred in charge, and Mordred used the opportunity to try to make his position permanent.

Again, a truce was arranged, but that was broken when a knight slashed at a live snake (an adder) at the treaty conference, causing a riot to break out. The king is now dead, Guenever is a nun, and the terms of the Interdict include The Boss. Indeed, he learns that the doctors who ministered to Hello-Central and who told him that sea air was needed were servants of the Church. Thus, The Boss and Clarence make plans for a last-ditch effort to hold off the forces arrayed against them. They have fifty-two boys who are faithful; all of the others whom they had trained reverted to their former superstitious ways when the Interdict was announced. Clarence has prepared a cave, fitting it with a dynamo, wires, and other similar supplies. In addition, if the end seems to be approaching, Clarence and the faithful will blow up all the factories and other institutions which The Boss has had built, so that these cannot be used against them; in addition, they have planted explosives in strategic places.

In front of the cave, they have rigged electric wire fences, and they have Gatling guns arranged to cover the entrance of the cave and the area beyond it. They also have torpedoes. Everything is ready, and so The Boss decides that they should take the offensive. He and Clarence declare the country to be a Republic, abolishing the monarchy, the nobility, and the Church. Then they head for the cave.

The first thing which they do when they reach the cave is to vacate the factories. Then they wait.

It takes a week, but a large part of England, nobility and common men alike, begins to gather near the cave. As more and more people reach the area, the boys become uneasy about the fact that they might have to kill their own people, along with the gentry. The Boss points out to them, however, that the nobility will lead the charge; they will be the only ones who are on the receiving end of what they plan to do. This reassures the boys.

Finally, the knights charge. They hit the spot where the torpedoes have been set, and they are blown to bits. At the same time, an order is given and the factories are blown up.

Then, while they wait to see what will happen next, The Boss sends engineers to divert a stream within their lines in a way that it can also be used against their attackers if needed. Then, when nothing more happens for a time, he prepares a message to "the insurgent chivalry of England," offering them their lives if they will surrender and acknowledge the Republic, but Clarence shows him that it cannot be sent to them.

During the night, the knights approached the fortified cave. As the knights crept forward, the electrified wire fries them. In their armor, the knights passed the current along to whomever touched them, so that when the mass attack occured, all of the men who touched the fences or who touched men who had touched the fences were killed. Still, however, others crept forward, not yet having reached this point. When a large enough number of them were between the ditch and the fences, The Boss ordered the stream diverted into the ditch. The Gatling guns cut down many of the attackers, and the rest were drowned as they try to escape. In all, The Boss estimates that they kill twenty-five thousand of England's knights. He believes that they are now the masters of England.

The Boss proposes that they go out and help the wounded, if possible, and they do so, even though Clarence objects. The first man whom they try to help is Sir Meligraunce; he stabs The Boss, as The Boss leans over to help him. The wound is not serious; however, Merlin slips into the cave in the guise of an old woman and puts a spell on The Boss that will make him sleep for thirteen centuries. Clarence, unfortunately, wakes up in time to see only the end of the spell and cannot stop him. Merlin, however, gloats about what he has done, brushes up against one of the wire fences, and dies.

As a last tribute to The Boss, they find a place in the cave where no one can bother his body, and they place this manuscript with it.

Then the original narrator, the one introduced in "A Word of Explanation," finishes reading this manuscript at dawn. He goes to the room of the stranger and finds him delirious, calling out for Sandy and Hello-Central. Gradually, his mutterings become more and more incoherent. As the end nears, he starts up and says, " 'A bugle? . . . It is the king! The drawbridge, there! Man the battlements!— turn out the—' "

"He was getting up his last 'effect'; but he never finished it."

Commentary

Chapter 39 begins The Boss's onslaught on the entire concept of knighthood, and it also reveals his monomania to destroy all of the institutions of Camelot – not just knight-errantry – but the nobility and the Church, as well. Chapter 39 also presents The Boss's attack against the knights. First, he takes the pageantry and makes fun of it by being dressed in tights rather than in armor. Then he rides a small, fast horse with great flexibility instead of using a huge, powerful steed. Instead of attacking, as was the proper form, he subverts the entire system by dodging rather than charging, and by using a lasso rather than a lance. The undignified manner in which he downs Sir Sagramor further shows the absurdity of the entire duel or joust.

After The Boss has made a farce out of the joust by roping several more knights, and after he has been deprived of his lasso, he has to face Sir Sagramor without a weapon, a most unknightly attitude on the part of Sir Sagramor; thus, Twain inserts another undermining of the nobility of knighthood. The scene where The Boss pulls out his recently made pistol and kills Sir Sagramor, then, explains the bullet hole that was in the armor in Warwick Castle in the opening section entitled "A Word of Explanation."

The final blow to knight-errantry lies in the absurd challenge that The Boss makes to all five hundred of the knights. As they charge, and he starts shooting with both guns, we have an absurd, imaginative picture of the Western cowboy firing into the overdressed and plumed knights, and when nine of these men are killed, the others immediately make a cowardly retreat, which reveals the final indignation of knighthood. In short, knighthood is made to seem utterly and absolutely ridiculous. An entire way of life is destroyed: "The victory is perfect – no other will venture against me – knight-errantry is dead."

Thus, with Chapter 39 and until the end of the novel, the book takes an amazing turn. In Chapter 40, for example, during the lapse of three years, The Boss is well onto his way of destroying the nobility and the Catholic Church and offering in its place democracy and universal suffrage "given to men and women alike."

Then, in Chapters 40 and 41, The Boss discovers that he has been tricked by the Church to take a voyage out of the country, thus allowing the Church to announce the Interdict. The indication, therefore, is that the Church is opposed to the advancement of civilization, and as Twain has pointed out elsewhere, the Catholic Church has often resisted advances in civilization.

Chapter 42 again tests the reader's credulity. In The Boss's absence, so much has happened in that short period that it is impossible to respond to it. The sixth-century aristocracy was made into railroad conductors, the Round Table became a stock exchange, admirable people such as the noble Sir Launcelot, the most noble of the knights of the Round Table, began to manipulate the stock market. Very shortly, jealousy and greed broke out among the knights leading to England's being divided into two warring camps — Arthur's and Launcelot's. The lovely, idyllic Camelot exists no more; instead, the greedy materialistic nineteenth-century America is now rampant throughout the country.

The last stand is made in, ironically, Merlin's cave. Here, the preparations that have been made for warfare again exceed our imaginations. In the chapter entitled "The Battle of the Sand Belt" (Chapter 43), the entire forces of The Boss consist of the fifty-two youths that The Boss has been able to train from childhood. The others that he trained were too old to withstand the superstitions of the Interdict. Nevertheless, the scientific advancements of the nineteenth century are too powerful for the simple knights of the sixth century. They have no way of withstanding mines, electrified fences, or Gatling guns; consequently, we have a devastation and death of such magnitude that it can only be accounted for by the ingenious inventions of modern weaponry. The peaceful beauty of ancient Camelot has been destroyed by modern, destructive weapons, and at the end of the battle, "twenty-five thousand men lay dead around us." Yankee ingenuity has won over knighthood, and The Boss acknowledges that from his own men "the applause I got was very gratifying to me."

The victory, however, is a Pyrrhic victory. The dead bodies of the 25,000 slain knights form an insurmountable barrier around the cave, and they are trapped inside their magnificent victory. The bodies begin to rot and putrify and in the process, victory begins to poison the victors one by one.

In Chapter 44, it is Clarence, not The Boss, who sums up the predicament: "We had conquered; in turn we were conquered."

This same sentiment is repeated by Merlin: "Ye were conquerors; ye are conquered!" The Boss is put into a deep sleep, and in the final Post Script by Twain, we find Twain (or the original narrator) entering Hank Morgan's room to find him ranting, calling out for his lost land, his wife, and his child. Thus, in the final view, The Boss is defeated *not* by Merlin, but by the methods of nineteenth-century war, commerce, and destructive weapons. Ironically, in the end, The Boss is more interested in returning to his happy life in the beautiful and idyllic land of innocence that he destroyed than he is in returning to the nineteenth century.

CHARACTERIZATION IN *A CONNECTICUT YANKEE*

In traditional terms, there are no characters in *A Connecticut Yankee*: there is only Hank Morgan. The other characters who appear are only pawns who serve to reflect some quality of Hank Morgan's. For example, Clarence appears more than any other secondary character in the novel, and we know that Clarence grows physically from a young page ("he was hardly a paragraph") to a fully mature man in charge of all of the Yankee's operations, but we are aware of only his chronological development. Or else, Hank Morgan and King Arthur travel together for eleven chapters, but we never really get to know the king; he remains a distant, shadowy figure, completely undelineated.

Hank Morgan is an ingenious, inventive Connecticut Yankee, filled with practicality and common sense, believing in complete democracy, opposed to the Catholic Church, and possessing a disdain for royalty and nobility; he finds knight-errantry to be absurd and childish. Thus, we have Hank Morgan, champion of nineteenth-century democracy, commerce, industry, progress, and science, placed in a society that is controlled by heredity, aristocracy and a dictatorial church and infested with unjust laws, injustices, and inhumanity.

While acting as the champion of the modern, nineteenth-century view, Hank Morgan's main attitude is his desire to show off. His love of an effect, his eye for the stage value of a matter, and his wish to perform picturesquely are all directly related to his indignations and his prejudices.

Because he has a more advanced knowledge of technology and because he has been exposed to thirteen more centuries of advancement, and because he knows how to do ingenious things, such as make gun powder, build a locomotive, and set up a telephone line, Hank Morgan immediately assumes that he is a superior being: "Here I was—a giant among pygmies, a man among children, a master intelligence among intellectual moles; by all rational measurements the only actually great man in the whole British world." It is his belief that because he is technologically more knowledgeable than other men, he is superior as a human being; this leads Hank Morgan to attempt to change, improve, and "civilize" Camelot, but in the process, he destroys it.

While acting as the champion of the modern, nineteenth-century view, then, Hank Morgan becomes essentially an unscrupulous opportunist who is more concerned with bringing personal glory to himself and in controlling other people than he is in actually improving the lot of mankind in general. Beginning with his first "miracle," Morgan is intent that the center of all attention must be constantly focused upon him. Most of his actions are performed for the purpose of self-glorification and personal gain. For example, when he performs two of his great "miracles"—the blowing up of Merlin's castle and the restoring of the Fountain of Holiness (using Greek fires and Roman candles for the effects), he makes sure that there are large numbers of people there to appreciate him and his efforts. He craves attention and is always on the lookout for the "theatrical effects" that he can achieve in his performance.

Yet while disdaining superstitions, especially the many superstitions that the Church has burdened the common people with, Hank Morgan constantly uses the superstitions of the common people to gain power for himself. In this way, he does not differ significantly from the Church—which he disdains. Ultimately, the long tradition of the Church and its control upon the superstitions of the people defeat Hank Morgan when it announces its Interdict. At this time, the people whom Hank has trained revert back to their religious and superstitious ways; ironically, they have seen Hank Morgan's scientific inventions *not* as science but as some new sort of *magic*. Thus, Hank Morgan's power is gained through superstition, and he is also defeated by superstition.

It should be stated, however, that Hank Morgan possesses real humanitarian concerns. He does not understand fundamental nature sufficiently to be able to respond to the real needs of the people of Camelot, but he believes that if he technologically provides a better soap that the people will become a cleaner people spiritually. However, one doesn't clean the *inner* soul of a people by washing the outer layers of the skin. While Hank Morgan is opposed to all types of injustice (all precedence given to heredity, to nobility, to a dictatorial church, and to all non-humanistic matters), yet he is not sufficiently educated to appreciate that the souls of people need to be changed gradually. And even though Hank Morgan is an advocate of progress, a man whose views, attitudes, and intentions are to be admired, yet his personal flaws—prudery, lack of insight, and desire for self-glory—cause him to become the "evil invader" of the innocent and idyllic land of Camelot. This, in turn, was responsible for Twain's later saying of Hank Morgan: "This Yankee of mine has neither the refinement nor the weakness of a college education; he is a perfect ignoramus; he is the boss of a machine shop; he can build a locomotive or a Colt's revolver, he can put up a telegraph line, but he's an ignoramus, nevertheless."

QUESTIONS FOR REVIEW

1. What is the function of the use of the "frame" around the story of Hank Morgan?

2. Discuss the two opposing views of knighthood that are presented in the novel.

3. What is Hank Morgan's view of the nobility, of the Catholic Church, and of aristocratic preferment?

4. How does Hank Morgan use his technological knowledge to gain power?

5. How well does power set with Hank? That is, does he use his power for the betterment of the people or for the glory of Hank Morgan?

6. What features of Camelot does Hank Morgan find attractive? Why does he try to change these aspects?

7. What is Hank Morgan's views on superstition? Does he ever use superstition for his own advantage? Explain.

8. How does Hank's nineteenth-century prudery affect his views about Camelot?

9. Which aspect of the novel do you consider more important—the social criticism, or the science fiction fantasy?

10. Discuss Hank Morgan's total failure to modernize Camelot in terms of his inventions, his attention to human needs, and his own prejudices.

SELECTED BIBLIOGRAPHY

PRINCIPAL WORKS

The Celebrated Jumping Frog of Calaveras County, and Other Sketches, 1867.

Innocents Abroad, 1869.

Roughing It, 1872.

The Adventures of Tom Sawyer, 1876.

A Tramp Abroad, 1880.

The Prince and the Pauper, 1882.

Life on the Mississippi, 1883.

Adventures of Huckleberry Finn, 1885.

A Connecticut Yankee in King Arthur's Court, 1889.

The Tragedy of Pudd'nhead Wilson and the Comedy of Those Extraordinary Twins, 1894.

The Man That Corrupted Hadleyburg and Other Stories and Essays, 1900.

The Mysterious Stranger, 1916.

BIOGRAPHICAL MATERIAL

BROOKS, VAN WYCK. *The Ordeal of Mark Twain.* New York: E. P. Dutton, 1920. Rev. ed., 1933. An influential study suggesting that the moralistic pressure of family, friends, and American culture affected Mark Twain's genius.

DE VOTO, BERNARD. *Mark Twain's America.* Boston: Little, Brown, 1932. This book gained notoriety for its heavy attack on Van Wyck Brooks's book listed above.

FERGUSON, DELANCEY. *Mark Twain: Man and Legend.* Indianapolis: Bobbs-Merrill, 1943. An excellent biography.

HOWELLS, WILLIAM DEAN. *My Mark Twain: Reminiscences and Criticisms.* Edited by Marilyn A. Baldwin. Baton Rouge: Louisiana State University Press, 1967. An affectionate memorial by an old, loyal friend.

WAGENKNECHT, EDWARD. *Mark Twain: The Man and His Work.* 3rd ed. Norman: University of Oklahoma Press, 1967. Originally published in 1935, this study is still one of the best.

CRITICAL WRITINGS

BELLAMY, GLADYS CARMEN. *Mark Twain as a Literary Artist.* Norman: University of Oklahoma Press, 1950. An early, full-length study of Mark Twain.

BLAIR, WALTER. *Mark Twain and Huck Finn.* Berkeley: University of California Press, 1960.

BRANCH, EDGAR MARQUESS. *The Literary Apprenticeship of Mark Twain: With Selections from His Apprentice Writing.* Urbana: University of Illinois Press, 1950. An account of Twain's early career.

CARDWELL, GUY A., ed. *Discussions of Mark Twain.* Boston: D.C. Heath, 1963. A collection of critical material.

COX, JAMES M. *Mark Twain: The Fate of Humor.* Princeton, N. J.: Princeton University Press, 1966. The author's thesis is that Twain's work was successful in his comic writings and unsuccessful in his serious writings.

DE VOTO, BERNARD. *Mark Twain at Work.* Cambridge, Mass.: Harvard University Press, 1942. The volume contains three long essays about Twain.

LEARY, LEWIS. *Mark Twain.* Minneapolis: University of Minnesota Press, 1960. No. 5 in the "Pamphlets on American Writers" series.

LONG, E. HUDSON. *Mark Twain Handbook.* New York: Hendricks House, 1957. A summary of Twain's life, background, ideas, and reputation.

MARX, LEO. "Mr. Eliot, Mr. Trilling, and Huckleberry Finn," *American Scholar*, XXII (Autumn, 1953), 423-40.

ROURKE, CONSTANCE. *American Humor: A Study of the National Character.* New York: Harcourt, Brace & Company, Inc., 1931, pp. 209-20.

SALOMON, ROGER B. *Twain and the Image of History.* New Haven, Conn.: Yale University Press, 1961. The book covers Twain's historical ideas and writings.

SCOTT, ARTHUR, L., ed. *Mark Twain: Selected Criticism.* Dallas: Southern Methodist University Press, 1955.

SMITH, HENRY NASH, ed. *Mark Twain.* Englewood Cliffs, N.J.: Prentice-Hall, 1963. A collection of critical essays.

STONE, ALBERT E., JR. *The Innocent Eye: Childhood in Mark Twain's Imagination.* New Haven: Yale University Press, 1961.